T0165713

Be Positive

Be Positive

Even If It's Not Your Blood Type...
Your Life Will Change

Rich Wood

New York

Be Positive
Even If It's Not Your Blood Type... Your Life Will Change

Copyright © 2010 Rich Wood. All rights reserved.

No part of this publication may be reproduced or transmitted in any form or by any means, mechanical or electronic, including photocopying and recording, or by any information storage and retrieval system, without permission in writing from the author or publisher (except by a reviewer, who may quote brief passages and/or short brief video clips in a review.)

Disclaimer: The Publisher and the Author make no representations or warranties with respect to the accuracy or completeness of the contents of this work and specifically disclaim all warranties, including without limitation warranties of fitness for a particular purpose. No warranty may be created or extended by sales or promotional materials. The advice and strategies contained herein may not be suitable for every situation. This work is sold with the understanding that the Publisher is not engaged in rendering legal, accounting, or other professional services. If professional assistance is required, the services of a competent professional person should be sought. Neither the Publisher nor the Author shall be liable for damages arising herefrom. The fact that an organization or website is referred to in this work as a citation and/or a potential source of further information does not mean that the Author or the Publisher endorses the information the organization or website may provide or recommendations it may make. Further, readers should be aware that internet websites listed in this work may have changed or disappeared between when this work was written and when it is read.

Brief excerpts of *The Dancing Wu Li Masters An Overview of the New Physics* Copyright © 1979 Gary Zukav reprinted with permission of Harper Collins Publishing

Brief Excerpts of *The Tao of Physics* Copyright © 1999 Fritjof Capra reprinted with permission of Shambala Publications, Inc.

Jung, C.G.: The Collected Works of C.G. Jung, Vol. 10 © 1964 Bollingen`, 1992 renewed Reprinted by permission of Princeton University Press

Jung, C.G.; Synchronicity. © 1960 Bollingen, 1969 Princeton University Press (second edition), 1988 renewed PUP Reprinted by permission Princeton University Press

ISBN 978-1-60037-771-6

Library of Congress Control Number: 2010922730

Morgan James Publishing
1225 Franklin Ave., STE 325
Garden City, NY 11530-1693
Toll Free 800-485-4943
www.MorganJamesPublishing.com

In an effort to support local communities, raise awareness and funds, Morgan James Publishing donates one percent of all book sales for the life of each book to Habitat for Humanity. Get involved today, visit **www.HelpHabitatForHumanity.org**.

Dedication

This book is dedicated to my mom, the eternal optimist. She is the one person in my life that has *always* been a positive influence. She is no longer with us, but she inspires me still—to this very day. With that said, I pass along her words—this simple concept that can change your life… "You can do anything you put your mind to!"

Acknowledgements

Writing a book is an exercise whose success is based not only on inspiration, but also on the perspiration of the team of people that must all come together to accomplish such an undertaking. With that said I have to thank my good friend Jeff Aubery for the initial inspiration and continued encouragement to take on this challenge along with his wife, Patty Aubery, President of Jack Canfield Enterprises, author of many *Chicken Soup for the Soul* books, and my agent. Her support and guidance has been invaluable. I would especially like to thank D.D. Watkins, friend and co-author of the best selling *Key to Living the Law of Attraction,* whose tireless support in helping me edit the content of this book has transformed it into a far better product and I am grateful. I would also like to extend my gratitude and sincere appreciation to Morgan James Publishing and Mr. Rick Frishman for taking a chance on an "unknown and inexperienced" writer.

Finally… I want to thank my wife Mary… the real inspiration for the title of this book, and my children, McCall and A.J. They inspire me to wake up every day and work at being the best person that I can possibly be.

Table of Contents

Foreword
This book is the real deal!

I n *Be Positive... Even If It's Not Your Blood Type*, Rich Wood explains not only *why* positive thinking works, but *how* it works. He speaks from a poignant personal perspective about the amazing ability of the mind and spirit to overcome great challenges, and even to heal the body. He thoroughly explains the core energy that lies within each one of us and connects us to all energy that exists throughout the universe; offering us not only the scientific explanation of this vast energy network, but also incorporating the concepts of Eastern wisdom and philosophy that support similar scientific fact. He emphasizes the importance of positive thinking and being, and explains that our minds continually create and project a frequency of energy: one that embodies our thoughts, attitudes, and intentions, creating a wave of change not only within ourselves, but affecting our physical reality as well.

This book offers us an extraordinarily clear and comprehensible discussion about the science behind synchronicity and the law of attraction—one of the best explanations I have ever seen. In these pages, Rich builds upon an undeniable foundation of science and philosophy in order to explain our connections to each other and to the world around us. He encourages us to embrace our very real *sixth* sense—our "sense of connection," and proposes that through our individual heightened awareness we will begin to create a tipping point within the human race... an evolution in *global* awareness. I agree with Rich: I believe that we *can* change ourselves and change the world, one person at a time.

Be Positive is thought provoking, compelling, and informative. With his background in the fields of science and engineering, a love of Eastern wisdom and philosophy, a penchant for research and an extremely impressive business career, Rich has a uniquely balanced perspective, and he speaks from experience. He learned to harness and focus his own energy at a very young age, and he has used it to heal and transform his body and his life. The personal stories and vignettes in this book are inspirational and they offer clear examples of how we can all create the successes in our lives that we desire.

Rich has put this incredible energy to work in his own life, and changed the lives of those around him—and you can, too. Read this book... your life will change!

Jack Canfield

Jack is the co-founder and co-creator of The New York Times #1 best-selling Chicken Soup for the Soul *book series,* The Key to Living the Law of Attraction, The Success Principles, The Power of Focus, *and many more, He is also the founder of Self Esteem Seminars located in Santa Barbara, California, which trains entrepreneurs, educators, corporate leaders and employees in how to accelerate the achievement of their personal and professional goals.*

Prologue

I was a very inquisitive child. I remember taking apart and reassembling every clock, toaster and television I could get my hands on—much to my parents' consternation. It's who I was then, and it's who I am now. I just seem to have an inherent need to know not only *how* things work, but *why*.

As a "not so invincible" teenager, I experienced two separate and devastating accidents. Against all odds, I not only survived, but thrived. I learned at the relatively young age of fourteen just how strong the power of the mind can be, and by harnessing that power and energy I was able to heal my body—not once, but *twice*. The course of my life was forever changed. I learned a great deal from the experiences, and I began to understand the importance of being *positive*. The accidents were a major catalyst in my desire to learn more about the power we each posses to heal our own bodies. It wasn't enough for me to know that my mind was powerful… I needed to know *how it worked*. I began an earnest personal quest—a journey of science and spirit. For nearly thirty years I have extensively researched everything I could get my hands on in relation to the power and the energy that is within each and every one of us. I've studied not only the physiology, the quantum physics and the history behind the science, but also the philosophy, psychology and theology behind the scenes, and in particular—Eastern religion and philosophy.

Now, this research was *not* to the exclusion or detriment of my family, career or business. In fact, the very opposite was true: *every* aspect of my life has been enhanced, balanced and guided by what I have learned. This search for knowledge and insight has simply been a common thread running throughout my entire life.

This book is my attempt to share with you what I have learned over the years, and to expose the facts that validate the concepts behind the "law of attraction" which has gained much notoriety in recent times. I hope that the information contained within these pages will help you with your own journey and that you will find yourself empowered to create the changes you desire in your own life. My goal is to provide you with a basis for understanding the power of your thoughts, attitudes, and intentions; and through this understanding for you to embrace the ability you have to change your own life! We are all so much more powerful than we realize. I've learned in my own life that there are teachers and opportunities all around us—all the time. Our families, colleagues, friends, and every person we come in contact with— each one of them has something to teach us. Every single event that takes place in our lives is a moment *filled* with potential. Every challenge in life is an opportunity, and it is how we handle these challenges that ultimately determine who we are. Being positive is the best thing you can do for yourself and for those around you. It really *will* change your life—it certainly changed mine. Energy is the very essence of all that exists from the Earth to the heavens, validated by both science and spirituality which are bound together with a common goal: to learn the deepest truth about our reality... a truth known to each of us when we quiet our minds and listen with our hearts.

To see a world in a grain of sand
And a heaven in a wild flower,
Hold infinity in the palm of your hand
And eternity in an hour.

God appears, and God is light
To those poor souls who dwell in night,
But does a human form display
To those who dwell in realms of day.

William Blake

(Excerpted from Auguries of Innocence)

Chapter One
Accidents Do Happen

I t was a warm, sunny northern California day in early June. I had just graduated to the big leagues from middle school. I was reveling in the fact that school was out, I would be playing high school football in a few months, meeting lots of girls, and I had the entire summer ahead of me to swim and hang out with friends. Life was good, and at fourteen years old, I felt as though I owned the world. That day, all of my buddies showed up at the door, as usual, with towels in hand, right about mid-morning. The hot sun also seemed to attract my older sister Naomi and her girlfriends, whose only goal this summer seemed to be hanging out around our pool in their swimsuits working on their tans. My friends had uncanny timing, and while I would have liked to believe that I was incredibly popular—I knew their real motivation. They all thought my sister was gorgeous and so were her friends. I guess I couldn't really blame them—girls were pretty much all I thought about, too. Naomi, at fifteen, was only a year older than I was, but she was my best friend and my confidante. We hung out together, and talked for hours at a time about everything, but when she and her girlfriends were together, I was just her punky little brother. I knew the drill. Once the first day of summer arrived and her girlfriends showed up, there was no way I would ever be allowed to even set foot in the back yard. It was their territory—off limits for me, my friends, and definitely for our younger brother Greg.

I knew my friends wanted to hang out at our pool, but I really wanted to avoid an argument with my sister, and besides I always lost. When the younger brothers and their friends try to occupy the same space with the older sister and her friends, it's like mixing fire and gasoline. So, when my buddies showed up ready to swim, I just told them that I had lost pool privileges for the day because I hadn't finished my chores the previous night. Instead, we headed down the street to Mike's house, he had a pool too; one of those doughboy types that sit on top of the ground. Just fine with us, we had a football, our radio, and the sun was hot. Mike's pool wasn't one of your normal above ground pools—it was customized. They had modified it by digging a big hole in the ground for a deep end and added a makeshift diving board. The pool was close to their house and to an adjoining fence, so there were ample perches from which we could make amazing leaps and dives, each of us attempting to outdo the other with the biggest splash. After an hour or so of cannonballs and belly flops, we shifted from "biggest splash of the day" to "football interception." We were all planning to try out for the football team in the fall and each of us, of course, thought we were the most talented. The game we played was one where you would dive straight out into the pool, from any point: roof, fence or side of pool and try to catch the football as your friend passed it to you. The goal was to catch the ball as far out as you could, as though you were catching the winning touchdown pass… and it was my turn!

After a few failed attempts, I climbed back up on the fence for another shot at imaginary football stardom. With a tremendous push off of the fence, I leaped—my arms outstretched as far as I could get them. The football came from the right, so I turned in mid-air and reached for the ball. My body contorted and twisted as I tried to make the catch, but I missed. The football sailed right through my fingers and I hit the water head first, far short of the deep end with my arms twisted to my side—definitely *not* the preferred entry in the shallow end of the pool! I shot straight down to the bottom of the pool like a bullet. I felt a thud on the top of my head, and remembered feeling stunned, but aside from that, nothing too unusual. I bounced off the bottom of the pool, my momentum carrying me back to the surface. I recall trying to kick and swim to the top as I had done a million times before, but this time… nothing. I was shocked to discover that my arms and legs weren't working and yet it didn't occur to me that I was really hurt. When my head finally came above water I managed to get out a brief call for help as I grabbed a quick breath of air and sank back below the surface to the bottom of the pool.

After what seemed like an eternity, (in reality it was probably less than a minute) I floated back to the surface, completely dazed but aware enough now to know I was in serious trouble. I couldn't move my arms or legs at all. I yelled for help again and grabbed another quick breath as I sank back beneath the surface. My friends realized then that I wasn't joking around. They jumped in, grabbed my arms, and pulled me to the side. Reggie and Bud lifted me out of the pool and sat me on the edge of the doughboy, holding on to my arms and propping me up so that I wouldn't fall backwards into the pool. With my head flopped over to one side, I was now keenly aware that something serious had happened. I asked Mike to run down the street and get my parents. My entire body felt as though it was vibrating, like holding one of those tuning forks you use for tuning a piano.

After a few minutes my parents came running into Mike's backyard. Fortunately, my mom had completed her nurses training program just a few months earlier, and upon hearing about what had happened, she had immediately suspected a broken neck. As soon as they reached me, she turned to my dad and very calmly told him to go and get the family station wagon; they were going to rush me to the hospital. She tried not to alarm me. "This will be faster than waiting for an ambulance," Mom explained. She sent Mike into his house to get an ironing board, and she stabilized my head with her hands. She knew that to prevent any further twisting or injury they needed some kind of rigid support for my back and neck, so she and my three friends laid me flat on the ironing board. I was beginning to go into shock, and was still confused as to what was really happening. The car showed up, and at first the ironing board wouldn't fit, but somehow they managed to get me loaded into the back of the station wagon without dropping me.

My dad was in the Navy and he felt the best place for treatment would be at Oak Knoll Hospital in Oakland, California, even though it was more than an hour away. My mom held my head steady the whole time and tried to keep me calm. I lay in the back of that station wagon staring up at the ceiling, not knowing really how seriously injured I was. I remember thinking that I might not be able to make tryouts for the football team at the end of the summer, and telling my parents several times how sorry I was for hurting myself. Mom tried to keep the conversation light, telling me that I was going to be alright, and not saying anything about how badly hurt she really thought I was. My dad was entirely focused on getting us there as quickly as possible and he maneuvered the station wagon through freeway traffic, around corners, and through the streetlights as we raced our way to the hospital.

The drive to get there felt like an eternity to me. The pressure of my mom's hands on either side of my head was all that I could feel. By then I was starting to get pretty nervous. I still couldn't move anything from my neck down. I had no idea what I had done to myself. We pulled into the driveway of the emergency room, my dad jumped out of the car and yelled to the waiting attendant, "My son is in the back and I think he just broke his neck!" Hearing that... I thought to myself, "*Okay, now I'm scared!*" The tailgate of the station wagon swung open as doctors and nurses swarmed around the car. Two doctors climbed in the back of the car as several others stabilized my head and neck, and together they gently lifted me out. They slid a real backboard beneath me, strapped my head down, and carried me into the ER. A flurry of activity ensued as the doctors checked my vitals, poked and prodded my arms, legs, fingers and toes. The attendants were checking for feeling and sensation in everything they could prick with a pin. They were careful not to alarm me as they quickly worked to come up with a preliminary assessment but it must have been obvious to them right from the start that my neck was broken.

At fourteen years old, I had thought of myself as invincible, yet here I was, and for some reason I couldn't move or feel a thing below my chin. I was wheeled down the hall to the X-ray room and draped with a lead apron. The technicians tried to reassure me that I was going to be okay, but this was a military hospital where they typically told it like it was and their reassurances weren't very convincing.... I suspected that they were shielding me from the severity of my injury. After dozens of different camera shots, all from different angles, I was wheeled back to the emergency room to await the verdict. I laid there flat on my back staring up at the ceiling, alone with my thoughts. Part of me still hoped that this was just a minor injury—that I would get a scolding from the doctors, to "think before leaping next time" and I would be sore but fine in a few days. In the back of my mind I was worried though… something was definitely wrong. While I could still breathe, talk, and move my eyes, there was this vague sort of vibrating sensation in my chest and I couldn't really feel anything else. It was the strangest feeling—like when you sit in one position for a long time and your leg falls asleep.

The doctors came into the room and huddled just out of earshot in the corner going over the X-rays. I could see by the shaking of their heads and stern look on their faces that I wasn't going to be heading home anytime soon. My parents were brought in and the doctors confirmed our worst fears—my neck was broken. Not only that, but my spinal cord was severely pinched and distorted where it wound its way through the center of the vertebrae that were oddly compressed together. The technical term they used was a "compound fracture of the cervical vertebra." They showed us the X-rays and proceeded to explain the injury. I learned that there are seven cervical vertebrae in your neck, the first one being the axis (the vertebrae your head sits and rotates on) plus six others leading down to the thoracic vertebrae (chest area) and on to your lumbar vertebra in your lower back. Somehow, the bottom of my third cervical vertebrae was compressed onto the *top* of my second cervical vertebrae! My spinal cord was twisted through the two compressed vertebrae like a pretzel, but it looked as though it might possibly still be intact according to the X-rays.

The doctors on staff were amazed that the vertebrae could be compressed that severely without *completely* severing the spinal cord. The compression of the cord between the vertebrae was shutting off all nerve function through the spinal cord—much like a kinked garden hose prevents water from flowing through it. Even as experienced military doctors, they had never before seen an injury quite like this. The staff doctors called for the chief neurosurgeon that was on staff that afternoon. As it turned out, the chief neurosurgeon was Dr. Kemp Clark, the very neurosurgeon from Texas Southwestern University that was called upon in the emergency room on November 22, 1963, when President John F. Kennedy sustained fatal gunshot wounds to his head. Dr. Clark was on rotation through Oak Knoll Hospital as a visiting doctor, and just happened to be on duty when I arrived in the emergency room. Looking back on it now, it was quite a fortunate coincidence. I was in very good hands.

Frightened and scared, I laid there, unsure of what was to happen next. A few minutes later, Dr. Clark showed up. He walked into the room, didn't say a single word to me, asked a few questions of the attending doctor, looked at the X-rays, and told them to immediately prep me for surgery. Although a bit short in the way of bedside manner, he was reputed to be a brilliant neurosurgeon. The head of orthopedic surgery at the hospital, Dr. Applegate, arrived to explain the plan. He told my parents and I that there was only one real shot at relieving the pressure on my spinal cord. They would have to place me in traction and then allow some time for me to stabilize over the next several days. The process would involve drilling holes into my skull, then screwing bolts into those holes. The bolts would connect to an 'ice tong' device, which in turn would be connected to weights." "The weights," he explained, "will pull on the top of your head—separating the vertebrae, and hopefully the traction will allow them to re-set to the proper location, like re-setting a compound fracture in your arm, for example." He also went on to explain the bad news: I would have to be fully awake and alert for the procedure, and it would be quite painful.

He said they were fairly sure that the traction would help relieve some of the pressure, but they were not confident that it would fix the compressed vertebrae. If the traction was not enough, they would have to go in during a second procedure to surgically de-couple the compressed vertebrae, and fuse the broken bones back together, essentially making the second through fourth vertebrae in my neck into one single vertebrae. This surgery would involve a much higher risk but would hopefully stabilize the fracture and relieve any remaining pressure on the spinal cord. Their primary concern was that the spinal cord could be severed in the process of de-coupling the compressed vertebrae. Given the complexity of the compression fracture and orientation of the spinal cord as it weaved through the fracture area, they feared that it may have been partially severed as a result of the injury already. The overall prognosis was pretty bleak. They did not know if I would *ever* regain feeling or use of anything below the neck—even with the surgeries. Again, this was a military hospital and they told it like it was.

My parents and I had to make a decision quickly, and we decided to take a chance and go ahead with the surgery. Some feeling and function was better than none, and besides—there weren't a lot of options to choose from. Within the hour I was wheeled into the operating room. They strapped me down, which was a bit confusing because I couldn't move anything anyways, and they draped a sheet over me. They reminded me that it was going to be painful and they told me to go ahead and scream if I wanted to—like I really needed encouragement! I was not given any anesthetic, not even a local one; I remained fully awake and coherent while they literally drilled into my skull with a power drill and what looked like your standard, everyday quarter inch drill bit. The pain while they were drilling into my head was beyond anything I have ever felt. They couldn't knock me out for the procedure because I had to stay awake and conscious so that I could let them know if they drilled too deep and hit something of importance... no joke. I could see the blood spattering the sheet that covered my face as they drilled, and I remember them talking to me throughout the whole process. Once the holes were in my head, they "threaded" them and screwed the bolts in tight. I must have looked like a teenage Frankenstein. When they were done, the doctors attached the ice tong looking clamps to the bolts on either side of my head, and then strung weights to the arms of the clamps. This contraption was attached to a bed that was suspended in the middle of two giant circular tube rings. This round device allowed them to rotate the bed 360 degrees so that they could keep me immobilized, but still rotate my body to keep my organs functioning. This bed was to become my prison for the foreseeable future. The objective of the traction was to relieve the pressure on the spinal cord by pulling my head and body in opposite directions, much like those medieval torture devices you've seen in the movies.

My parents were allowed to come in and see me once I was alert and coherent after the surgery. They hadn't seen the circular bed, the bolts in my shaved head, or the traction device connected to the weights, so they were definitely in for a bit of a shock. My poor dad took one look at me, his face turned ghostly white, and he spun on his heels—running out of the room and down the hall crying. Mom was a little bit more stoic, but she was crying, too. It's hard to see your parents like that, I recall feeling even more terrible for having caused them so much pain.

It was a Thursday morning—and five long, difficult days had passed since the accident. Meanwhile, my arms, hands, legs and feet had become virtual pincushions. Every time the doctors came in they pricked all of my extremities to see if any feeling had returned. On this day they did all of the usual tests, but this time something was a little different. I was able to *feel* a few of the doctor's pin pricks, but they didn't really hurt, it was more like just pressure on the bottoms of my feet... the traction was helping! I had been trying to come to grips with the reality and the severity of my situation, but I was still having a hard time accepting the possibility that the condition I was in could be permanent. That little bit of feeling in my feet gave me renewed hope, and my spirits improved somewhat, but the doctors took much more of a "wait and see" approach.

My family visited me as often as they could, but Dad would usually be the one to stay home with my younger brother, so my mom and my sister became my cheerleading team. Mom was the quintessential optimist—she consistently bolstered my confidence and insisted that I would be out of the hospital soon. I was getting pretty used to the hospital routine by the end of the first week. The nursing staff came in to rotate me in the circular bed every few hours. Since I couldn't really feel anything there was certainly no need for pain medication. The staff and doctors were always joking around with me and trying to keep my spirits up. I was able to eat, although I didn't have much of an appetite, and besides, the food was horrible. All I could really do to occupy myself was watch the television when the bed was rotated just right, and listen to the radio. I was *completely* dependent on the nurses. Whatever I needed; a drink of water, changing the channel on the radio or TV, I had to wait until someone came in my room in order to ask for their help.

I was normally very independent, so this was *not* easy for me. Since I couldn't turn my head, I was forced to lay there and stare at the ceiling (or floor) for hours at a time. The days were getting longer, and the nights seemed to last forever. All I could do was lay there and think. The possibility of what my future might look like was starting to sink in. I couldn't keep the "bad" thoughts out of my mind—I was starting to allow myself to think that maybe this *was* a permanent condition. I tried my best to block out the negative thoughts, but as the days went by with no news from the doctors about what might happen next, and with so little improvement, my spirits began to sink again. I began having nightmares at night, dreaming that I would fall out of bed onto the floor and my head would stay bolted to the bed with the weights dangling.

By the end of my first full week in the hospital I would anxiously await visiting hours. I was lonely, scared and miserable—I missed my life, my friends, my home—everything. *Was I going to ever get better?* Dinner (if you could call it that) came and there I was, with bolts in my head hanging from this giant contraption, being spoon fed my meal by one of the nursing aides. Imagine for a minute, here I was, a fourteen-year-old boy, hormones flowing, and I was being spoon fed my cherry Jell-O by the nurse's aide. It was not one of my finer moments. As they were clearing the trays my mom arrived, big smile as usual, explaining that my dad had stayed home with my brother and sister to clean the house. A reasonable excuse except that I don't *ever* remember seeing my dad clean the house. I think it was just too much for him to see me like that, or maybe Mom wanted to talk with me alone. I guess I had reached my mental limit and I broke down crying. The fear inside of me had been building and I just couldn't see how things were going to get any better. I didn't understand why this had happened to me, why was I being punished like this. I told my mom about the nightmares I was having and confided to her that I was really getting scared. For the next hour or so she tried to comfort me. She explained that medicine is an inexact science. That sometimes doctors don't have all the answers and sometimes, injuries just can't be fixed. As she spoke I could tell that she was also concerned by the fact that I hadn't shown much progress. She was trying to keep me positive, but at the same time I knew she was also beginning to prepare me for the worst. The reality was that I could very well end up being a quadriplegic for the rest of my life… my greatest fear.

She also caught me up on daily life back home and what my friends were doing, to get my mind off the subject. Then she smoothly shifted into one of her little pep talks (life lessons she called them) that she would give me whenever I was faced with a challenge in my life. My challenges up to this point had never amounted to more than passing a test or asking a girl to go to the dance with me. This time was definitely different. "Everything happens for a reason honey, you just don't know yet what that reason is," she said. Mom reminded me that *I could do anything I put my mind to*, the very words I had heard thousands of times growing up… I was raised on those words. She said, "However this injury ends up you can make the best of it, don't let this get you down. You've never given up on anything before so don't you *dare* start now." She made a quick transition into "drill sergeant" mode and told me that I was tough and that I *would* come through this little test, and that if I wanted to walk again then it was up to *me*. She told me (in no uncertain terms) to *quit being negative, think positive thoughts, and make it happen!* She reminded me that the power of the mind is the strongest force in the world, and that people have been known to do amazing things—like healing their own bodies, overcoming devastating injuries, or using super human strength to pull someone from a burning car. She reminded me that I was in a Navy hospital, one that had seen its share of American war heroes many of whom had survived incredible injuries, far worse than mine, and have gone on to do great things with their lives.

After she left that evening, I pondered her words; *I can do anything I put my mind to*. At fourteen years old, it was hard for me to relate to this—was she trying to say that I could *think* my way out of this hospital bed? How? My bed was angled in such a way that I could gaze out the window and see the stars in the night sky. It was quiet, and I was alone with my thoughts. In that moment I decided I would *not* continue to just lay there and feel sorry for myself. I *could* choose how I was going to let this accident affect me. The accident happened for a reason, and while I might not understand what that reason was, the simple fact was: *it happened.* I couldn't change the past, but maybe I *could* change my future. I could either drown in self pity being spoon fed Jell-O for the rest of my life, or I could try to *do* something about it. *I decided that I would beat this injury and that I would get out of this bed and walk out of the hospital on my own two feet.* I had absolutely no idea how I would accomplish it, and I had no clue if it was even medically possible—but for some reason the act of making that decision, that *commitment* to myself, made me feel like I had a chance. Like there was hope.

My thoughts were interrupted by the new night nurse. Her name was Sherry. She was young, fresh out of college, very cute and she smelled good. I always looked forward to the night shift change. I might be in pretty bad shape, but I was still fourteen years old and girls were still one of my top priorities. She was friendly and she always lifted my spirits and cheered me up. She rotated the bed and swung it around to face the television, then turned it on for me and tuned it to a special that was on about Eastern religious philosophies and monasteries. Sherry smiled at me over her shoulder as she left the room to tend to her other patients and her wonderful perfume lingered, as the door closed behind her. As she left, I turned my attention to the television and absorbed myself in the show's story line. It was about a group of young boys who set out to join the monastery. Their path was a journey of self discovery gained through meditation and self sacrifice, leading to the attainment of an enlightened state of awareness. I was immediately intrigued—they talked about how many of the monks had developed tremendous control over their minds and bodies through deep meditation, allowing them to accomplish miraculous feats of mind over matter. Some of the concepts the monks talked about, it seemed, weren't all that different than what I thought my mom was suggesting. *You can do anything you put your mind to.* These monks were being taught the very same thing in their monasteries! It was exactly what I needed to see and hear, at exactly the right time. Looking back on it, this was probably the beginning of my fascination with Eastern philosophy.

I finished watching the show just as it was time for lights out. Sherry reappeared in my room to turn off the television, and gave me a sleeping pill to help me sleep through the night, a new (and much appreciated) routine given my recurring nightmares. I remember thinking, as I lay there waiting for the effects of the pill to overpower me, about the coincidence of this show... this story line... the concept of meditation... and my mom's pep talk that I could do anything I put my mind to. I knew there was a message or an answer for me there somewhere—something that would help me get through this. It just hadn't dawned on me yet how to put it all together. *What was the key to make it work?*

By the middle of my second week in the hospital my injury had stabilized and the swelling around the vertebrae and spinal cord had gone down. The feeling hadn't improved much and I was still unable to move anything, so the decision was made to go ahead and perform the second surgery. Dr. Clark came in during afternoon rounds to let my parents and I know that the surgery was scheduled for the next day. He explained the whole process and talked to me about what to expect. He also made a point of reminding me that I could still come out of the surgery with permanent spinal cord damage and that it might take weeks before we would really know if it had worked at all. Dr. Clark was very direct; he wasn't one for building false hopes. In his words, "It would turn out however it turned out."

Needless to say getting to sleep that night was nearly impossible. I was awakened the next morning just as the sun was rising, prepped for surgery, and wheeled off to the operating room. I was terrified, but determined to be as positive as I could about it.

Seven hours after the surgery I woke up in the recovery room—still in my circular bed, still attached to traction, and to my horror still not able to move or feel anything from my neck down. I immediately thought the worst; that my spinal cord had been severed during the surgery! I was in a weird half awake, half asleep, drug induced state that made everything feel dreamlike, but I do remember waking to my parents being there and reassuring me. "Everything went fine," Mom said, "It's all done, now the rest is up to you!" and I fell back asleep.

Dr. Clark and Dr. Applegate both came by several hours later after I was fully alert. They told me that the surgery went as well as they could have expected. They explained that they had used a little crowbar to dislodge the two coupled vertebrae and that my spinal cord, to their surprise, appeared intact. Dr. Applegate even tried joking with me, saying, "I even think we got your head back on straight." I guess I wasn't in the mood for humor—I don't remember smiling. "Just kidding," he said. "We did have to pry the vertebrae apart, they were really stuck together," he explained. "Then we reinforced your vertebrae with the bone chips that we cut out of your hip." Dr. Applegate went on to say that over time this bone would fuse across the first three vertebrae in my neck making the fractured second, third and fourth vertebrae act as one single vertebra. "It will take several days or maybe a week before the swelling goes down enough for us to determine the extent of any permanent damage to your spinal cord." Dr. Clark said.

I was out of the ICU and back in my room in a few days, still a bit loopy from the pain medication, but fully alert and aware of what was going on. My parents, brother and sister bounced into the room with big smiles to cheer me up. Naomi had made me a bologna sandwich with mayonnaise and mustard, my favorite; knowing how much I had grown to hate the hospital food. I was relieved to have the surgery behind me, and eager to start working on the next stage of my rehabilitation, whatever that was. The visit with my family was short, but sweet. I was tired and the nurse came in to rush them out so I could sleep. Mom hung back for a few minutes as the rest of my family left. She picked up my limp hand and reminded me, "You can do anything you put your mind to, you know that right?" She said. "It *is* within your power to heal and get up out of that bed and walk again. If you want it badly enough you can make it happen—you always have in the past and this is no time to change. *You can do this Richard*, I know you can." She kissed me on the forehead, turned around and left the room to join the rest of the family down the hall. As the door closed behind her I thought about what she had said. I reminded myself that I could make this happen. *It was up to me*—"*I can do this,*" I said to myself as I drifted off to sleep.

My bed was angled just right, and I still couldn't move anything, so I spent the next day looking out the window just daydreaming and thinking about what I was going to do first when I was out of there. Dr. Applegate came in to check on me in the afternoon by himself, and instead of a quick visit (as most of them were) he sat down beside my bed. We talked about some details of the surgery, and about how the healing process would work. He gave me a "mini" lesson on anatomy, and explained how the spine and spinal cord work together, and told me about the regeneration capacity of the nerves in the spinal cord. Naturally, I had a *lot* of questions for him. Recalling the television show that had been on the week before, I asked him if he happened to know anything about Eastern religions and their concepts of "mind healing body." As it turned out, he had actually studied various elements of Eastern medicine and Eastern religious philosophies during his training overseas.

He explained to me how the medical and philosophical beliefs are much more connected in the East than in the West. "The West tends to treat medicine more as a process, treating separate parts of the body, running lots of tests, not really an exact science, more like symptomology," he said. "We're still learning about the body all the time." He described how in Eastern regions medicine treats the "whole body" considering mind, body and spirit as completely connected. "The powers of the mind have been shown to accomplish amazing things,"… "and these incredible strengths have been demonstrated many times in Eastern countries." He said. I told him more about the television show I had seen, and explained how the monks used meditation to tap into their own inner strength and power. He indicated that he had seen this sort of thing firsthand during his military training, and he said that Western countries (like the United States) were just beginning to explore the concepts of treating the "whole" body. "Holistic Medicine" he called it. Dr. Applegate described his own experiences with meditation techniques and suggested that I give meditation a try. "The important thing to do," he said, "is to channel all of your positive energy to the area of the injury and visualize the healing of your nerves and bones. Visualize yourself walking again." He finished up our conversation by telling me to get plenty of rest, encouraging me to remain as positive as I could and reminding me that I could make the best of *whatever* happened.

As I watched him walk away it dawned on me that the Eastern philosophers had indeed discovered something very important. It seemed to me that the strength of the mind and spirit were probably just as important in the healing process as any medicine, surgery, or science that might be used to fix or repair an injury or illness. It made perfect sense. I spent the rest of the afternoon thinking about our conversation and reflecting on what I could remember of the television show. The feats achieved by those monks seemed to be the result of spending many years practicing meditation. I certainly didn't intend to spend years laying in this bed waiting for a miracle, but then again, I certainly had nothing else going on— so why not give it a try?

That night I tried some of the meditation techniques the doctor had suggested. It was after dinner, the night shift staff was on duty, and evening rounds were done. I could count on several hours of no interruptions. I closed my eyes and forced myself to relax. I focused on my breathing, in and out, slowing the pace down each time I exhaled, just like Dr. Applegate had suggested. As I exhaled, I concentrated on going further and further into a relaxed state of mind. Well… it sort of worked I guess. The next thing I remember, it was midnight and Sherry woke me up to rotate my bed. I must have drifted off to sleep—I don't think I was supposed to do that. It was a less than auspicious beginning, but I certainly had plenty of time on my hands to practice until I got it right.

The next morning the sun was shining; the nursing staff and everyone around me seemed to be in positive spirits. After morning rounds and breakfast I tried my meditation again. This time I knew I wouldn't drift off to sleep. I closed my eyes, again focusing on my breathing. Each time I exhaled, I slowed my breathing further and let myself fall into a deeper state of relaxation. I felt my body relaxing in "waves" with each breath I exhaled. I knew it was working. I heard noises in the room and outside my doorway—yet at the same time I felt detached, aware only of my thoughts. I focused harder, trying my best to block out the noises and turning my attention inward. I visualized a point inside my forehead that would get increasingly smaller as I slowed my breathing and I was keenly aware of my heart beating. I could sense the energy building inside of me. Eventually, when the only awareness I had was of the spot inside my forehead, I shifted my thoughts and the point of my concentration to my neck; the bones, the spinal cord and nerves. I tried to visualize tiny red blood cells, like little soldiers, full of healing energy, all rushing to this one area from all over my body. I was mentally moving the energy that circulated through my body. The process I used was basically a combination of both meditation and visualization.

I spent the rest of the week (every uninterrupted chance I had) practicing this technique. I gradually increased the length of time that I could remain focused, and I concentrated all of my positive energy on healing my bones and spinal cord. In the beginning it took me quite a while to get to a level of relaxation, where I was able to block out the external noises and focus my concentration. With time I found that I was able to achieve a relaxed state in a shorter amount of time—usually within just a few minutes, and I could stay focused much longer. By the end of the week I had worked my way up to three good sessions a day of at least an hour each. I was feeling alive with energy, and I was positive that something would soon change.

Friday rolled around, and in the late afternoon the door to my room swung open and Dr. Clark walked in. He barely spoke as he went about his now familiar exam. He pulled out this three inch long needle from his coat lapel to poke and prod various parts of me—the old pincushion routine. He got to my feet, and to my shock and delight I thought I could feel the needle prick the bottom of my feet! This was something that I hadn't felt at all since the second surgery. I told him I was sure I felt *something*, so as a test he told me to close my eyes and tell him which foot he was poking. "My left foot," I said, "now my right." I felt a very dull pressure like something on the bottoms of my feet, not quite the painful prick from a pin that you would expect, but something undeniable as a sensation. I was elated. Finally three weeks after my accident, and almost a full week after the second surgery—*real progress!* Dr. Clark was excited too, but in a much more "cautiously optimistic" way. He indicated that while this was certainly a positive sign, we still needed more time to see whether or not the progress continued. There was still a ways to go in the healing process… but I knew that the meditation, the focusing of all of my energy on healing my injury, and my positive attitude, were working. This was my validation. It gave me hope and increased my level of determination to work even harder at my meditation. I knew I was going to make this work. Every day I focused on one single goal; to get up from that bed and walk again.

I think that was my turning point in the healing process. Over the course of the next week I accelerated my efforts and worked my way up to two or three hours of meditation and visualization at a time, several times a day. I kept getting better at it, and every day I could feel more and more sensation in my extremities. By the middle of the fourth week, I was even able to move my toes, feet, fingers and arms; *and* the feeling throughout my body had started to come back. By the end of that same week

I could move my arms, legs and hands. Everything seemed to be working again! The doctors and nursing staff were thrilled by my progress, and amazed by the level of change they were seeing in me on a daily basis. Dr. Applegate commented that this case was surely one for the medical journals, as he had never seen such rapid progress in this type of injury. Normally spinal cord injuries take months or even *years* to heal, if they heal at all! Rarely do such injuries recover fully. I was absolutely convinced that my remarkable progress was direct proof of the power of the mind. I believed in myself, I believed that I could heal my own body, and I felt empowered that I could control my own fate.

It had now only been five weeks since the accident. I had my feeling back and was able to move everything again, but I was still in traction and still connected to the circular bed. Physical rehabilitation was added to my daily routine to rebuild the strength in my arms and legs. I had lost nearly forty pounds in a month, and I looked a lot like a cross between Frankenstein and a skeleton. Now that I was able to move my hands and lift my arms I could read again, and Dr. Applegate had brought me an assortment of books on Eastern philosophy and religion that I was really looking forward to reading. Lying on my back made it virtually impossible to read for more than a few minutes, so one of the nurses brought me some prism glasses that allowed me to hold a book on my chest and actually read it. While laying flat on my back, looking towards the ceiling with these glasses on, I was able to read the pages. After so many weeks of staring at the floor or the ceiling—it was a much welcomed change of pace.

I continued to meditate three or four times a day, fully convinced that this was the reason I was healing so quickly. I was literally willing myself and my body to recover. Now that the feeling in my arms and legs had returned, I actually had to concentrate even harder on relaxing all of my body to get to a focus point where the energy was centered. I pictured myself floating in the air, suspended above the bed, blocking out all of the sensations of my body. As I progressively moved into a deeper state I could almost feel and see the energy flowing and pulsating inside my body, warming and glowing brightly where I focused. I concentrated all my thoughts on increasing blood flow and energy, and I visualized the nerves and bones healing. I could actually feel it working! I had also become the center of attention at the hospital for visiting doctors and medical students, and would often entertain small groups of student doctors. Dr. Applegate and Dr. Clark would stop by often, always happy to "show off" the results of their fine work. With each day I was more and more convinced that I really *had* found the key to achieving virtually anything I set my mind to. I discovered an internal strength that I knew would enable me to overcome any adversity.

My progress had been so substantial by then that I was custom fitted with a unique neck brace that allowed me to finally be removed from traction. The plastic brace ran from the top of my head to just below my ribcage. It would also allow me to resume many of the more normal activities—like walking, while keeping my neck supported until the muscles and bones in my neck further strengthened and healed. I was excited to get out of that bed and stand up. I had been flat on my back for five weeks, but I assumed that I would be able to just slide my legs around the edge of the bed, jump down on the floor and take a short walk. It wasn't quite that simple—I was about to receive a few quick lessons on anatomy and physics. The nurses rotated me in my bed to a standing position. With the doctor in front of me and a nurse on each side supporting me under each arm, I tried to take a step forward. I moved my foot from the bed to the floor, but as soon as I put weight on my leg it was like there was absolutely nothing there to support me as I collapsed towards the floor. I could move my legs but had little or no muscle left in them to support any weight. They lifted me back to a full standing position but I couldn't stand on my own, I just couldn't balance and my head started spinning. I was shocked that I had forgotten how to stand up and walk, and even more surprised that I had lost that much strength. "Don't worry about it Rich," Dr. Applegate said, "This is entirely normal." Because of the injury to my spinal cord there may have been some residual nerve damage that could make it difficult for me to walk or stand. I couldn't believe it, I thought once all the feeling had returned that I would be able to jump out of bed and start walking right away, and sadly this wasn't the case.

Even more determined now to prove that I could do this, I resumed my regime of meditation and physical therapy. Working several times a day, trying to stand and walk, I was building the strength in my legs and upper body that would also help with my balance. I made rapid progress. Within a few days I *was* able to stand on my own and take a few awkward steps. I visualized myself running again. My strength was returning, but I still had a long way to go. It was now nearing the end of my sixth week in the hospital. My spirits were high and I was surrounded by my family, friends and the staff at the hospital all of whom encouraged me every single day. Dr. Applegate and Dr. Clark were astounded at the radical change in my condition and even more amazed by the speed of my progress. Obviously, they were proud of themselves for the job they had done, but I think they were equally proud of me for not letting the injury beat me down.

The two of them came in during rounds that Friday afternoon. It happened to be during visiting hours and both of my parents were there as well. The doctors told us that they had done all that they could for me. It was now time for me to go home and continue my work there. Perhaps some good old fashioned home cooking would help put a little bit of weight back on me, and the change of environment would be a good stimulus to continue my progress. "I think we can send you home on Monday," Dr. Applegate said. Everyone around me, including the doctors and nurses applauded. They had all been pulling for me from the very beginning, and I knew that they all wanted a happy ending for this skinny fourteen-year-old boy.

My family stayed with me that day until visiting hours were over. As they said goodnight with big smiles on their faces, I could see the relief in their eyes. I was coming home soon. My mom (as usual) hung back for a few minutes as the others walked towards the elevator. She kissed me on the cheek and quietly whispered, "I'm very proud of you, I knew you could do it. See… you *can* do anything you put your mind to!" She said. And with those words, she turned and walked out the door to catch up to the rest of my family. Visiting hours were over and I was alone again. I laid there gazing out the window towards the mountains in the distance. I took a deep breath, a sigh of relief. *I was going to walk out of that hospital on my own two feet*, come Monday morning… just a few days away. I was proud of myself. For a brief moment I reflected on my journey. I could never have imagined this experience. In many ways I felt like I had discovered "super powers." I was completely sure of myself and I knew I could do absolutely anything I set my mind to, ANYTHING! The summer sun was low on the horizon. I watched the birds flying along the canopy of trees that lined the parking lot below. People moved quietly along the street and sidewalk just outside the hospital, each in their own little world—completely unaware of the miracles that were happening around them. It was a surreal feeling. Not only had my body come through a tremendous transformation but so had my mind and spirit. I was a different person than I had been just six weeks earlier.

As I watched the sun slowly set, I realized that the key to my progress over these past weeks was in large part a result of my own positive attitude and determination, my willpower and my confidence that I *would* be able to overcome this injury and walk again. It was, without question, a result of the power of my mind to heal my own body. At the hands of medicine alone, and with no active intervention by me, I suspect the results would have been much different. However, by directing my own internal energy, through meditation, I was able to focus the healing energies of my mind to the parts of my body that were injured. With clear focus, I visualized the healing that would lead to getting off my back and walking again. I was surrounded by positive people with positive energy, and I managed the flow of my own energy to aide in the healing process. Above all, I believed in myself relentlessly. I knew I *could* do anything I set my mind to.

Did I end up walking out of the hospital? Of course... the weekend went by in a blur and Monday morning arrived. I was consumed with the excitement of going home. The doctors and nursing staff all came in to bid me farewell. The nurse brought in a wheelchair to take me to the front door, I said my goodbyes to the staff, thanking them for all that they had done for me, and off we went. The nurse wheeled me right up to the door of the hospital and then she stopped. I took a deep breath, stood up, and walked out that door on my own! With a smile on my face and my mom, dad, brother, and sister at my side, I walked out those doors on my own two feet. Dad had the station wagon waiting at the curb. I climbed in and was finally homeward bound! I had learned a great deal in the past few weeks—lessons that would serve me well in the months and years ahead.

Looking back on the events surrounding the accident, I can now fully appreciate the roles of coincidence and synchronicity. I do not consider "coincidences" to be entirely random or meaningless intersections of people or events—but rather, quite the opposite. The people that came into my life at just the right time, and the luck that I had… I can't help but think that these coincidences helped to provide me with the guidance, inspiration and direction I needed along my journey. If circumstances had been different, I would be in a very different place right now. My mom going to nursing school to fulfill her lifelong dream; the choice of what hospital to take me to, and Dr. Clark's coincidental visiting tour at Oak Knoll Hospital at exactly the same time I was there. There were also some pivotal events that served as catalysts for major shifts in my state of mind. Mom's pep talk a few days after the accident—reminding me that I could do anything I put my mind to, and the television show about the Eastern religious philosophies, and how the monks developed their capacity to control the power of their minds through deep meditation. Finally, Doctor Applegate's firsthand experience in treating the mind and soul as one, and his opening up with me and sharing his knowledge of Eastern medicine, meditation and philosophy. These "coincidences" provided direction in my life at just the right time, and had they not occurred, my journey would have gone in a completely different direction.

So here are a few thoughts that I think are important to remember. We go about our lives facing decisions every single day, and our decisions affect our lives and the lives of those around us. Our lives follow a path that is determined by the choices we make, and sometimes these choices take our lives in a direction we could never have imagined. We all have the ability to change our own lives, and that change begins with us, in our own minds. If we want something out of life we need to go get it! When we are clearly and intently focused on our goals, then our energy is channeled towards achieving that goal. Whether your goal is healing an injury or getting a promotion at work doesn't really matter. Decide what it is you want to change or work towards, believe in yourself, and make it happen. It's important to pay attention to coincidences in our lives when they occur. Believe me, nothing happens by chance. The people we meet, we meet for a reason. It's up to us to be open to these coincidences so that we might understand the direction or guidance they may provide.

I remember asking myself "Why me? Why did this accident happen?" It occurred to me much later in life that I was asking the wrong question. Accidents happen. They are part of life. The real question, from the very beginning was, "How was I going to deal with it?" I was faced with tremendous adversity at a fairly young age, and while I had the best doctors, my future reality depended in large part on how I chose to deal with it. When we're faced with great challenges in our lives, the choices we make will determine the outcome and ultimately establish our failures and our successes. I learned that by facing adversity with a positive attitude and knowing that I could affect my own reality with the energy I had deep inside of me, I could overcome almost anything.

Chapter Two:
The Power to Heal Yourself

I t was early August when I returned home from the hospital and only about six weeks before I would be heading back to school as a freshman in high school. Although I was weak and I tired easily, my spirits were high. I still had to wear my brace for another eight weeks or so, as the bone grafted into my neck healed. I had a lot of work ahead of me but I was ready to charge ahead, armed with a new sense of confidence, energy, and purpose; eager to take on whatever lay ahead.

My family helped me set up an exercise routine that included walking, weightlifting, swimming and a *lot* of eating. Everyone took turns working with me. We didn't have a weight set, but we improvised with a set of old encyclopedias that served quite nicely. I was so weak that I had to start with the "D" and "E" volumes; the thinnest of the whole set. I would lie on the ground and with my arms stretched out to my side, one book in each hand, I would attempt to raise them up. I couldn't even lift them for the first few days, but I kept at it. Swimming was equally difficult. Before the accident I could swim for hours, and now I couldn't even float. I started by holding on to the side of the pool and kicking to build up my leg strength. My mom and sister would stand in the pool with me and hold me in a floating position on my back while I did my arm and leg exercises. In just a few weeks my strength increased considerably. I was up to weight lifting the "G" through "J" volumes of the *Encyclopedia Britannica*, could swim a few laps, and walk around the block without having someone standing next to me. I ate like a heavyweight wrestler in training and ended up putting on about twenty pounds in the first three weeks! I continued my meditation daily—focusing my energy on the continued healing of my nerves and spinal cord. By the end of the summer I had returned to hanging out with my friends, who helped me lift real weights and worked with me in the pool to build up my stamina. Reggie, Bud and Mike had all made the high school football team, and I worked out with them in their garage, a few houses down the street. My visits with the doctor showed continued improvement, and all of my neurological functions were nearly back to normal. There was virtually no sign of the injury at all, and the brace that I wore became a requirement only when I slept. Life had pretty much returned to normal and I was supported in my full recovery by both friends and family.

September rolled around and off to school I went, without the brace and looking about as normal as a fourteen year old can look. By then you couldn't tell by looking at me that I had been injured at all. My weight was back to normal and I was actually stronger than I was before the accident. I was finally able to start running again. I was back to feeling fairly invincible and since my injury was almost fully healed; I no longer felt the need to continue my meditation ritual. I fell right back into the habits and attitudes of any normal teenager. By the end of October I was officially given a clean bill of health from the doctors. I no longer needed to wear the brace at all and my only limitation was that I couldn't do any contact sports—so football was definitely out of the question. Considering the alternative, this was a small price to pay.

I turned fifteen that winter, and the accident, the paralysis, the surgery, and the weeks spent in the hospital were already becoming just a memory—one that faded more with each week that passed. I was a typical high school freshman with nothing but girls and sports on my mind. I tried out for the high school track team as a medium distance runner, and made it. Family life was normal; my spare time was spent chasing girls and harassing my younger brother and older sister. For all intents and purposes I had completely put my broken neck behind me. Aside from the scars on the back of my neck and my hip, there was absolutely *no* residual damage from the injury that occurred less than six months earlier. It really was a miracle.

Time passed quickly and before I knew it spring had come. It was early May and summer break was just two short months away! My sister Naomi and I were still close, and we still hung out together pretty often. She was a high school junior that year, and her boyfriend Ross was a senior. Every once in a while they would include me in their outings. On one particular afternoon they were just hanging around at our house and decided to go out for hot dogs. I was playing basketball in the front yard and they invited me to tag along. I didn't hesitate, and I jumped in the backseat of Ross's car (a very cool 1967 mustang) on the passenger side behind Naomi and off we went. Ross was a good driver and we were only going a few blocks away from home on residential streets so I didn't bother to put my seatbelt on. Pulling out of the driveway is the last thing I remember about that drive.

The next memory I have of what happened was like being in an eerie dream. I could hear people's voices and the sound of sirens going off. I was looking *down* from the top corner of what seemed like a very small, brightly lit room; and in that room my sister and I were both lying on cots, with people rushing around us. The people were yelling to each other over the loud sounds of what seemed like sirens, and the room was rocking back and forth, forcing them to brace themselves against the walls of the room. I simply observed what was happening.... I was the spectator in this "dream" and yet I was watching myself from this bizarre vantage point above it all. It slowly dawned on me that we were both inside an ambulance, lying next to each other and there were medics working on each of us. One moment, I was calmly looking down at the two of us lying on the cots (not making the connection that they were actually stretchers) while the medics worked on us furiously.... I remember feeling a sense of bewilderment, I wanted to call out to someone, but I couldn't. I wanted to wake myself up from this strange dream but I couldn't seem to do that either, and then all of a sudden I was back in my body with a jolt! I bolted upright, terrified. The EMT that was working on me pushed me firmly back down to a flat position. "You've been in a car accident," he said, "and you're hurt pretty bad." "My sister?" I asked. "She's right here, she's pretty bad too." He said. His voice was brusque, but he did offer some words of comfort. "Relax, you're going to be okay—we're headed to the hospital now." That's all I remember. I don't know exactly what had happened in those moments that I was looking down at us. Had I died for a moment and then come back? All I know is that I became an observer for that instant, and that I existed *outside* of my physical body. I felt no pain, and I felt no fear. I fell unconscious again and drifted in and out during the ride to the hospital.

When I woke again it was in the emergency room. Opening my eyes, I looked up and saw bright white overhead lights, and faces hovering over me that were covered in white masks.

I remember laying there terrified that I had re-injured my neck. "My neck?" I asked, "Did I hurt my neck?" I'm sure I was in shock, but at that moment I couldn't feel my arms or legs at all. "Your neck looks okay," a nurse said, as she started to cut off my brand new 501 Levi's. I vaguely remember asking her not to cut them off—they were my brand new jeans, but then something clicked and I remembered Naomi. I asked the nurse where she was and if she was alright. "She's here too, but we don't know how badly hurt she is. She's in the other room," The nurse replied. I must have drifted off again, because that is all I can remember.

My parents had been called and when they arrived at the hospital they were told by the emergency room doctors about the severity of our injuries. The doctors didn't expect either one of us to survive the night. Naomi had suffered a severe head injury in the accident and was in a coma. I was a little more fortunate, but all of the ribs on my right side were broken; my right lung was punctured in several places, had collapsed, and was filling up with blood. I had severe internal injuries, *and* my back was broken. The only good news was that it didn't look like I had re-injured my neck. At that point we were both in the Intensive Care Unit and the doctors were doing all they could for us.

That day and the days that followed must have been sheer hell for our parents. My sister was still in a coma and the doctors still feared that my internal bleeding and injuries would grow worse, but they couldn't do anything for me until my condition stabilized. It was two days before I turned the corner and fully regained consciousness; I had no memory of the accident at all. When I did wake up, my mom and dad were there by my side and they told me what had happened. Apparently we were about a block from the hot dog place when the car we were in was hit broadside by another car full of high school kids that were out goofing around. They had run a stop sign, slamming into the passenger side of the Mustang we were in—the side where my sister and I were sitting. Naomi had her seatbelt on and the impact thrust her head straight up into the roof of the car, causing massive head injuries. I was in the backseat right behind her, and I was thrown up against the roof and then over to the far side of the car behind the driver. The impact crushed the entire right passenger side of the car. I was lucky. If I *had* been wearing a seatbelt I would have been cut in half by the metal torn from the frame of the car. Fortunately, my sister's boyfriend, Ross, was uninjured and nobody in the other car was hurt either. "Naomi has a bad head injury and she's in a coma right now. She hasn't regained consciousness," Mom said. Her eyes were red and puffy. I remember crying—afraid of what might happen to my sister. "Is she going to be okay?" I asked. "We don't know honey," she said, "we're going to have to wait and see."

The next few days were a blur and I was drifting in and out mentally most of the time, trying to come to grips with what had just happened. I was in tremendous pain; my body hurt all over and it felt like someone was sitting on my chest. The attending doctor came in and explained that my lung was not re-inflating on its own because of the internal bleeding, and they would need to put a tube in my chest to drain the blood. He walked out of the room and returned with a nurse, surgical tools, and a big jug that looked like one of those large water bottles. "This is going to hurt a lot," he said. He then instructed the nurse to stand by my left shoulder and hold me down. I watched as he numbed my upper right chest with Novocain, and then took his scalpel and literally punched a hole right through my chest and all the way into my collapsed lung. I was fully alert and awake for this whole procedure—I didn't even get a minute to consider what he was about to do, he just did it! He inserted one end of a quarter inch plastic tube into the big glass jug, and the other end into my chest. He stitched the tube to my chest and that was it, done in twenty minutes! I was now physically attached to the large glass jug sitting prominently on the side of my hospital bed. The doctor said my lung should re-inflate after the blood in my chest was drained. I would have to stay attached to this jug for a week or so—long enough for all of the internal bleeding to stop. The bruised internal organs and my back would also heal with time. He told me that the healing process was now up to me and that in time I should fully recover. *Here we go again—déjà vu. "The rest was up to me." I had heard these same words before—just nine months earlier.*

Throughout those first few days in the hospital I wasn't given any details about the severity of my sister's injuries. I was only told that the doctors were doing all that they could, that she was still in a coma, and had not regained consciousness. My mom and dad were there constantly. My brother was shuttled off to friends and neighbors because he was too young to be there and had to go to school. My parents spent as much time as they could at the hospital, splitting up work and hospital shifts, so at least one of them could be with us as much as possible. They tried to split their time between my sister and me.

Despite the tragedy my parents and brother were dealing with, they somehow still managed to remain positive. I knew how hard it was for them to see both of us in so much pain. My mom still gave me her little pep talks. She continued to remind me that I could do anything I put my mind to, and told me that I had surprised everyone by walking out of the hospital after breaking my neck, and by God, I could overcome this injury as well. But somehow this injury seemed so much worse; my whole body hurt, I was drained physically and mentally and worried sick about my sister. Mom looked drained, too. She spoke the words with her usual conviction, but I could tell that deep down she was having a hard time being positive and believing them for herself with all that had happened.

Here I was, in the hospital again, and in really bad shape. I was worried about Naomi and I couldn't imagine life without her. I wished that there was something that I could do for her, but all any of us could really do was to wait and hope for her to regain consciousness. It was just after breakfast and I was alone, left to contemplate what had really happened just days before. I laid there looking out the window, once again wondering: *Why me? Did I have some curse? Was this all my fault?* Just then my mom popped her head in the room—perfect timing as usual. My head was pretty messed up with these thoughts, I was concerned about my sister, and I was pretty depressed. I confided my thoughts and fears to her and she tried to console me by explaining that this was just a freak accident. She assured me that it had nothing to do with me and she tried to shift the focus of my thoughts to the positive. She reminded me that the accident and injuries could have been so much worse, and how lucky I was that I hadn't re-injured my neck. She told me that my only job now was to get better—that was what my sister would want—she would *not* want me laying there feeling sorry for her—*or* for myself. She explained that getting better and getting out of the hospital would certainly take some emotional pressure off of the family. My little brother Greg missed me, too. I wasn't doing anyone any good lying in the hospital when I could be home. Mom's visit was short, she spent as much time with me as she could, but she really did need to spend time with Naomi too. The nurses told me that Mom would sit and talk to her for hours at a time as though my sister could hear every word she said, even though there was no outward sign that she was even aware of her presence. I have a feeling that she was sitting there with my sister, giving her the same kind of advice and encouragement, just in case she could hear her. As she got up to leave she reminded me again that I needed to focus on getting better. She told me to stop feeling sorry for myself, *think positive and make it happen.* I remember crying as she left. I felt scared and helpless, I hurt, I was lonely, and I was far more worried about Naomi than about whether or not I could overcome these injuries. It just didn't seem right to focus on myself when she was just down the hall in far worse condition.

After she left, I laid there thinking about all that she had said. I felt emotionally raw, but I realized then and there that my mom was entirely right, and I changed my attitude that moment. Naomi would definitely be the first one to give me a swift kick in the butt if she saw me wallowing in self pity like this. I knew my dad and brother, as well as my friends would expect more from me, giving up was not a characteristic of my personality; I didn't want to let any one down.... I didn't want to give up on myself. *Okay, so how do I find something positive in this mess?* I was basically chained to this huge glass bottle connected by a long tube that was stuck into my chest. I could barely move, with all my ribs and lower back broken, not to mention my whole body (inside and out) bruised—I wasn't going anywhere anytime soon, but I was alive and I was out of intensive care, and *that* was something positive.

I realized that I had to get focused on getting out of that bed. I knew how to do this. My goals were clear; get the tube out of my chest, get walking again, and get home. This time the challenge seemed even tougher than before, probably because my whole body hurt so badly. I knew what had worked for me before, so I started my meditation regime again, but blocking out all of the noise inside and outside my head and getting into that focused, relaxed state, was much tougher than before. Each time, I closed my eyes, all I could do was think about how much everything hurt! So, I just had to focus even harder and stay with it. I told the nursing staff that I wanted to rest so that they wouldn't disturb me. I would close my eyes and relax; starting with my toes, and moving up from there to the rest of my body. I relaxed my body in stages, breathing very deeply in and out, each time using the pain first as a point of focus, and then blocking it out. With some practice, I was soon able to again visualize a point behind the center of my forehead where all of the energy would center. From there I focused on moving the energy to my lung and healing my lung tissue. I envisioned the lung as fully healed. I then moved the focus of my energy and concentration from my lung to my broken ribs, then on to the vertebrae in my back, and finally to my liver and right kidney, the two organs that suffered injury during the impact. Each time I concentrated the healing energies on a single focal point, visualizing each injured area in the process of repairing the damage and then seeing them as fully healed. The whole process would take about two hours and I tried to do this several times a day.

By the end of my first full week in the hospital I was fully engaged in my old routine of meditation and I started to see improvement and feel better. I was also surrounded by the positive energy of my family and friends all rooting for me. My aunts and uncle traveled from back East to visit, and my friends from school would also come by. I wanted to get out of that bed as soon as possible. I knew I could do it and I could do it quickly; I had lived this and proven it to myself once already. I knew I could change my physical reality and speed up the healing of my own body by using the power of positive thinking. The key to creating the changes I wanted was to focus all of my energies on accomplishing my goals, visualizing my success, and working hard at it every day.

My lungs had shown improvement, and after eight days, the bleeding had subsided and the doctors told me the tube could come out. The same doctor and nurse came in to prep me. "This is going to hurt," he said again. This guy sure had a way with words. He positioned himself on my right and kneeled on the edge of the bed so he had an angle that allowed him to pull straight up. He cut the sutures that held the tube in my chest, grabbed hold of the tube and paused. "Take a deep breath," he said. And then he pulled *hard* on the tube. In one swift motion he pulled about a foot and a half of tube out of my chest. I let out a blood curdling scream (heard all the way down the hall and probably well into in the next county) and I swear it felt like the doctor had pulled my right leg up through the hole in my chest, along with my lung and my right arm. The pain was unbelievable, but the tube was out and all of the other pain I had been feeling was completely overshadowed by the pain I now felt in my chest. The doctor sewed me back up, told me I would feel much better in the morning, gave me a pain pill and then turned and left the room.

Within a few days, the doctors were ready to re-evaluate my overall condition. It seemed that my lung and internal organs had healed surprisingly quickly, but the broken ribs and vertebrae in my lower back were going to take a little more time. The doctors were astounded by the level of healing I had achieved in such a short period of time. The injuries I sustained would normally have taken several months to heal according to the doctors. The chest tube had been out for only two days, and already there was a huge improvement. They were amazed that I had made such rapid progress, and they told me that I would be well enough to go home the following day and continue my recuperation there. As the doctor was leaving he commented, "I have never seen a kid as lucky as you, to have come through two life threatening accidents in the span of less than a year; you must have some angels watching over you!" With that he turned and left the room.

So that was it, a total of ten days in the hospital and I was going home. My thoughts returned to my sister, my best friend, lying in a bed down the hall, still comatose. I couldn't imagine what she must be experiencing. There was nothing that any of us could do for her. She had to find a way out of that coma on her own. Part of me still wished that it had been me and not her sitting in the front seat. I wished that somehow she could have been spared. Another part of me was happy to be going home. I had no idea how long the road to recovery would be for Naomi, and I had no idea how long it would take me to get completely back on my feet, but I did know that I could do it; I had done it before and I could do it again.

The next morning came quickly. The doctor showed up as promised with signed release papers and some cautionary comments about my activities for the next month or two and then it was time to go. My departure from the hospital was bittersweet; I was excited, but a huge part of me and my life was being left behind with my sister still there. The trip home was quiet. I fought back my tears the whole way, heartbroken that Naomi was not coming home with us.

I stayed home from school for another full week and then it was time for me to return. My freshman year in high school was coming to an end. The routine at home wasn't great—everything was different. In between my mom and dad's work schedules they would spend all their spare time at the hospital with Naomi. She wasn't showing any signs of improvement, and some aspects of her health had begun to deteriorate. My brother and I went along sometimes but my parents tried to shield us from the pain of seeing her like that. When they came home from the hospital at night they were completely exhausted. Sometimes we ate dinner together as a family, but not very often. Our family life that summer was stressful, and my brother and I basically survived on our own. My parents didn't neglect us and certainly did what they could, but they were only human and seemed to get through it one day at a time. I continued to do my meditation, and had begun exercising again, burying myself in those routines. I had already made tremendous progress and the signs of the injuries from the car accident had all but disappeared.

A visit to Dr. Applegate confirmed that there was no further damage to my neck, and the fusion of the three vertebrae was now fully complete and healed. The range of motion and strength in my neck was perfectly normal. It was a miraculous recovery, according to the doctors, and they felt I was incredibly lucky to have escaped re-injuring my neck in the car accident. Another miracle… I had survived. I was sent home with instructions to keep doing whatever it was that I was doing, because it was working—again!

My body was in great shape, despite all of the injuries I had sustained over the past year. The meditation and exercise that I had structured my life around had shown great results. I handled the situation I was in by moving forward, setting goals and achieving them. My life, at least from the outside, appeared completely normal. Deep down, though, I was struggling terribly. People kept telling me I was "lucky," but on the inside I wasn't always so sure. I was trying to stay positive, but I was deeply conflicted by having survived both accidents and recovering as well as I had, while my sister was *still* lying in a coma in the hospital. A little more than a month had passed since the accident and I felt useless, unable to help her. I could heal my own body but I struggled with the fact that I couldn't help *her*. I couldn't find a path for resolving the conflicts in my head. *Why was I spared, why was I able to get better and why not my sister?* I questioned myself repeatedly, I questioned my parents, and I questioned God. No one had an answer.

There really wasn't an answer that anyone could offer that would make any sense to me; these were answers I had to find myself. Mom, in her great wisdom reminded me, "Everything happens for a reason. Our lives have a purpose, and sometimes it may take a long time to figure that out." She explained that people come and go throughout our lives to help keep us on our life's path. She also said, "Events occur in our lives for a reason, to either redirect us back on course, or to take us in a direction that will lead us to learn something that will be important later on. You don't know what your path is just yet, but you *will* find it." We had talked about these very same concepts before, but at the time I didn't fully understand what she meant.

In spite of everything, I was still only fifteen years old, and I was dealing with these tremendous internal conflicts that I was not emotionally mature enough to handle. As my body grew stronger, I had stopped my meditation practice—I didn't realize it at the time, but I guess I simply considered it to be a very useful "tool" for healing, and didn't think I needed to continue it any longer. Besides, I was feeling pretty invincible—I had clawed my way out of two dire situations—I was strong, I was healed, school was now out, and I had a lot of freedom to do as I chose with my parents gone so often. I sort of lost my "balance" at that time in my life, and while I was still extremely goal oriented, I was also "acting out" a great deal—taking foolish risks and being a daredevil—just taunting the cosmos to go ahead and take me. I was struggling to find answers to why all of this happened to me, to Naomi, and to my family. I was angry and scared, and Mom's words of wisdom just weren't enough. I knew my parents were worried about my state of mind, and they were getting pretty fed up with my reckless behavior. It was a really difficult time emotionally for all of us. Our lives had changed forever. I wasn't handling any of it very well, and I was wracked with guilt.

The next day was a Saturday morning. My brother and I were sitting eating our cereal watching cartoons, while Mom and Dad (as usual) were getting ready to head out to the hospital. My mom walked in the room and calmly announced that they were going to send my brother and me back to Michigan to my grandparent's house on Wiggins Lake for a month. We would be leaving on Wednesday. Greg and I looked at each other in astonishment, wondering what we had done so terribly wrong that we were going to be sent away for a whole month. This was a pretty big trip she was talking about; all the way across the country and we had never even been on a plane before! She explained that it would be good for us both to get away from the situation at home, and to go enjoy some time fishing and swimming at the lake. Neither of us wanted to leave our friends for the summer, but nothing we could say would change her mind. Later that evening while I was sitting in my room listening to music, my mom came in and sat down on the bed. She explained that she was *really* worried about me and that one of the reasons she was sending us away was so that I could spend some time thinking about everything and getting my head together again. If I didn't come back with a better outlook on life, and a little more appreciative of the miracles I had been given, then she was going to send me to a psychiatrist.

The threat of seeing a "shrink" was as bad as the classic threat of being sent off to military school, and I knew she was serious. So, Wednesday rolled around and off we went. I was pretty confused about many things. I knew my mom was right; I did have some issues to work through and being at home under the circumstances, wasn't helping. Spending time at the lake with my brother and grandparents, contemplating all that had happened to me over the past year, would perhaps bring some insights or answers. Worst case scenario, I could get a tan, not have to clean the house and maybe even meet some girls! In the end it turned out to be just what I needed and in spite of the circumstances—a pretty great summer. I did get my head straight, got my priorities set, and matured… with time, distance and some healthy distractions I gained some perspective on the accidents and knew what I had to do.

It's been more than three decades now since those accidents. Naomi did regain consciousness, coming out of the coma almost a year later, but she was severely handicapped. The doctors predicted that she would need to be institutionalized, but she (and my parents) proved them wrong. She was left with permanent brain damage from the accident, but she worked hard, and with the help of family, a lot of friends, the staff from the hospital, and perhaps even some divine intervention, she made great progress—regaining some use of her limbs and even her speech. Due to the nature of her injury her brain had to be retrained and "rewired" through exhaustive therapy and rehabilitation. Her intellectual functions remained intact, but her motor functions, speech, and everything else had to be relearned. It is amazing that she was able to regain all the function that she did. Naomi was confined to a wheelchair, but she still managed to go back to school and get her high school diploma. She even had a job for a while, but she spent her entire adult life at home where Mom and Dad took care of her every day until she passed away in March of 1998 after losing a valiant battle with breast cancer. She has always been an inspiration to me. In spite of everything she had been through, she still maintained a cheerful disposition, an easy smile and a witty sense of humor. She had a rough life, but she managed to remain positive every single day. She taught me more than I can say, and I miss her terribly. I have learned so much from my own family, including the importance of waking up each day and letting the people around you know how much you love them, because in an instant it can all be taken away— changed forever.

It's odd how the years pass so quickly. After the second accident I didn't really spend as much time at home as I used to. I tried to help with my sister, but I guess the pain of seeing her like that was just too much. I was grateful for the miracle of her regaining consciousness, but the reality of everything that had happened to her (and to all of us) was still pretty tough to cope with at fifteen years old. So, I just kind of moved forward in my own way. I drove myself to achieve one goal after the next, each one more challenging than the last, still convinced that I could do anything I put my mind to. I've heard it said that "almost dying can change your life." I couldn't agree more. I am sure that most people who have experienced such a thing would agree, but they would probably also say that after six months or so, their lives fell back into the same old routine. You see, even though coming so close to death changes you in a very basic, profound way, it is just too easy to fall back into old, familiar patterns and behaviors. What I learned is that while almost dying once will change your life for a while... almost dying twice, now *that* will change your life *forever!* Although so much time has passed, the lessons I learned that year shaped the course of the rest of my life. There isn't a day I wake up without feeling grateful to be alive.

Over the years I have continued to set goals and achieve them. My horizons were drastically expanded at a young age, and to this day I continue to actively expand my comfort zone on an ongoing basis. I am fearless to a certain degree, and I thrive on facing challenges (business, personal, you name it) and overcoming them. This self-confidence, positive attitude and strength have certainly contributed to my business and financial success as well. Understanding the power of the mind has enhanced every single aspect of my life. The lessons I learned in my youth were deeply ingrained in me and became an integral part of who I am. I was empowered by the experiences and challenges I faced, and I knew I could do whatever I set out to do in the world. I am positive to a fault perhaps, and sometimes it drives my family nuts, but I do know this... be positive, despite your adversities, and your life *will* change.

Chapter Three
Hidden Lessons in Adversity

L et's face it; no one's life is free from adversity, but there are always hidden lessons in adversity if you are open to learning them. I've definitely had my share of "opportunities for learning." I believe that it's these very challenges, the adversities we face in our daily lives and how we deal with them that define us in many ways. Ultimately, our choices and how we deal with our challenges make us who we are and define our character. During that summer on the lake I learned a lot about myself, and even more about how I was going to face life from that point on. I remember lying on a raft in the middle of the lake for hours each day pondering the circumstances that led up to the accidents, and wondering why I seemed to be fated on a path of destruction. Laying there listening to the wind blowing through the trees, feeling the warm sun on my face, and gazing up at the clouds floating quietly overhead, I waited for an epiphany. I wanted some answers, needed some direction. Well, there wasn't any grand epiphany that summer, but those quiet introspective moments were an essential part of my emotional healing. I wasn't particularly religious, but I definitely felt I had been granted two incredible miracles. I suppose looking back on the accidents, I easily could have assumed that I was spate with a run of bad luck and that the third accident, just around the corner, would be the "strikeout." Instead, I chose to look at the positive side of things. There was no way two freak accidents like that should have occurred so closely together—and yet I had survived both of them with no real permanent physical damage! Emotionally I was still dealing with the repercussions, but physically it was almost as if the accidents had never happened. Miraculous by anyone's definition. I thought there *must* be a greater purpose in life for me, to have been spared twice. The million-dollar question burning in my mind was: *What could that purpose possibly be?*

I guess I realized that I had some choices to make about how I was going to handle things from that point on. We *all* have choices in our life, no matter the situation or circumstances. We decide how we are going to deal with our challenges. We choose our path by the decisions we make when faced with our own adversities and our lives progress in a direction dictated by those decisions. I felt the challenges I had were really no more difficult than those many other people faced every single day, and the lessons I learned were profound.

There is no doubt looking back, that the power of my mind played a tremendous role in my miraculous healing. In both situations, the beginning of the healing that occurred started with a change in my own attitude, my *choice* to heal and get better, and my decision to take ownership of the direction my life was going to move. I knew intuitively that I could make things happen. Certainly the expertise of the doctors was critical to the process as well, but even they were floored by the speed and completeness of my recovery. We all have the same potential—I didn't do anything that you can't do. Was it a miracle, divine intervention, or the power of the mind and human spirit? Looking back, my recovery happened because of *all* of these things. I believe they are all one and the same: they are all just different forms of ENERGY AT WORK!

We have choices, and by choosing, we decide what path our lives take. We can certainly choose to do nothing at all when we are faced with issues or challenges in our lives, but with this choice the results are certain; nothing will change. Nothing ventured, nothing gained, right? Or, we can choose to try and overcome the obstacle, despite how overwhelming it may seem. In this way we set out on a path for ourselves that is one of our own choosing—and that path will lead to success. Your life, your decisions, your intentions and the choices you make determine your path, whether it leads towards success or failure.

I chose to seek out the purpose behind the events I had experienced, and I have dedicated much of my life to the quest for greater understanding of the power I discovered within myself—the power that is within each of us. I know… it's a little more ambitious than figuring out how the toaster works, but it really has been a goal and a driving force for most of my life. So, as I headed off to college, *science* was my field of choice. I knew that science held some of the answers for me and it was a subject that fascinated me…. I ended up attaining my Bachelors degree in Aerospace and Aeronautical Engineering from Michigan (Go Blue!) and my Masters degree in Aerospace Engineering from USC—two of the top engineering schools in the country. The educational choices I made led me to a career within some of the leading high technology companies in the world today and provided me with the opportunity to work alongside some of the most brilliant minds in the business. That particular career choice also segued into many other opportunities and successful business ventures as well. I also made a conscious decision to continue my journey into the depths of spiritual knowledge and understanding. Over the years I have studied philosophy, psychology and Eastern religion. My life has been shaped not only by my personality and the events that have taken place along my journey, but also by the choices I made as I matured and grew. Now science and philosophy may seem like diverse and different areas of study, but at their core they are far more similar than you would think. In short, I have chosen to study (from many different angles and perspectives) the *energy* that lies at the center of all things. I will do my best to share some of what I have learned with you here in these pages.

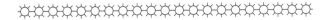

The mind has incredible powers, only a fraction of which we have even begun to tap into. When I was young I learned that through deep meditation I could focus this same energy (that we each possess) on the parts of my body that were injured. I used meditation to first establish a deep state of relaxation that allowed me to tap into a wellspring of internal energy, and then I focused this energy on healing those areas of my body. I was just a kid, obviously with no formal training or guidance in meditation, and at that time I simply used the technique for healing, unaware of the other benefits. In fact, the practice of meditation in the West, back in the early 1970's, was one that had been experimented with by only a few small groups—primarily as a carryover from the political activism and hippie movements of the 60's. I discovered much of my personal meditation technique by chance and experimentation, but I had time and the determination of youth on my side, not to mention some serious incentive to perfect it. I now realize that what I was actually doing through meditation was establishing a *synchronous frequency of energy* vibrating throughout my body. This harmonious energy was channeled, building in strength and ending at those single points I focused on. Initially it would take me almost an hour to get to the relaxed state where I could feel the energy pulsing through my body. Blocking out all of the noise outside my head was difficult enough, but quieting the noise *inside* my head was the greatest challenge. I called this process "quieting my mind." Over time and with practice, I found that I could quiet my mind more and more quickly. In these states of deep meditation the frequency of pulsing energy ebbed and flowed throughout my body in time with the rhythm of my breathing. As I continued to slow and control my breathing, I found my ability to channel and focus the energy increased as well.

Meditation was an important part of my personal healing process but it was equally important for me to set goals and *visualize* accomplishments. Visualization has proven to be an effective means of self-transformation, and training, and it is often utilized in different forms of research and analysis. It has been successfully used in a variety of different areas; including business, classroom, and sports applications. Olympic athletes use visualization on a regular basis as part of their mental training regime. Even NASA uses visualization for shuttle flight and mission specialist training purposes, and also as a means for interpreting large amounts of complex data "visually" (through simulation) in order to draw conclusions, make decisions, and communicate the results of their research and analysis.

For me visualization was a powerful tool I used every day to keep myself motivated and to aid the focus of my energy. I *saw* myself overcoming these injuries. I *saw* myself healed. There was no question in my mind that I would succeed, but staying focused on positive energy was hard, it took a lot of self-discipline and commitment. In addition to that, my energy from within also needed to be strengthened and supplemented with *external* energy. It was incredibly helpful that everyone around me encouraged and pushed me to keep on going. There were times when days or weeks would pass with little or no apparent progress, and whenever my energy would get low or I became discouraged, the reinforcing external energy came from the people around me.

Positive energy was contributed by everyone around me: the doctors, nurses, hospital staff, and most importantly, my family. Through their encouragement and positive attitude, they all aided in my healing. Their positive energy coupled with mine, and together created a sum that was far greater than the individual parts. I was told everyday that I could do anything I set my mind to, and that if I wanted to get better badly enough—I could make it happen. I heard these words, integrated them into my consciousness, and believed in them. I believed in myself. I believed in the positive energy!

Now, it's important to note that this same concept also holds true for negative energy. Be aware that if you choose to focus on the negative; if you have a negative attitude and convince yourself that you'll fail, regardless of the specific challenge or adversity, you are destined to fail. Not only have you set up a negative energy that works against you, your health suffers because your internal energy is being depleted on negative thoughts, and you attract other negative people into your life that feed upon your negativity and add to it. This increases the likelihood and probability of failure. If you think you are going to fail before you even try—then, guess what, you will indeed fail! When you accept and acknowledge that you can do anything that you set your mind to then you are establishing a positive mindset that creates a positive energy that flows from within.

This energy can then be strengthened both internally and externally through a combination of several things. Meditation is certainly a good way to increase the energy flow in order to overcome adversities such as health challenges, but it also works to create a better flow of energy within your body and creates measurable physiological changes; having the overall effect of creating a better, more positive mindset. If your mind and body feel good then you will have a much better likelihood of battling the challenges in your life.

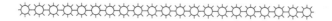

Goals are essential. My goals in the hospital were clear, they were easy to grasp, and they gave me direction, and provided a focus for my energy. For me it was pretty straightforward in the case of both accidents: Get up and walk out of the hospital on my own. Your goal may be overcoming an adversity or challenge in your life, resolving family or personal issues, a professional goal, or dealing with an illness. Regardless of the form it takes, the first and foremost step is to set your mind to achieving or overcoming whatever those challenges may be. Establish a positive attitude that you will succeed; feel it, know it, and believe in yourself—*believe* that you will succeed.

Defining your goals and objectives is a critical first step towards accomplishing them, whatever they might be. But just thinking about them isn't always enough. You can give your goals a life of their own and strengthen them by writing them down. I've counseled many people that have worked for me over the years to use goals and objectives as a process for growing in their careers. I have always said, "A goal isn't real until you write it down." Commit your goals and objectives to paper, and place them in prominently visible locations where you will see them regularly. I like to use index cards and tape them to my mirror and my computer monitor. Find what works for you and do it! If your goals are easily defined in pictures or images, then use those too. The next step is to visualize yourself achieving these goals, all the while believing in yourself and knowing that you can achieve them. The process of visualizing your success will begin to set up a positive frequency of energy within your body. This works to help push you towards achieving that goal and it helps to bring people and situations into your life that will contribute positive energy and aid in moving you closer to success.

Over time, I've become increasingly diligent about setting goals and objectives, and then working hard to achieve them. I still have one, three, and five year plans that get updated regularly. I am always assessing and reassessing my life in terms of my goals and objectives, and I have them all written down, I refer to them often and I modify and update them on a regular basis. I basically follow my own advice!

One of my passions is flying. I learned to fly many years ago, and ultimately became a flight instructor. As a Gold Seal flight instructor I have had the privilege of helping many people achieve their lifelong dreams of learning to fly planes and becoming pilots. But the process of learning to fly is challenging for most people. It requires a complicated set of skills and it involves developing both mental and physical muscle memory. Mental memory applies in the context of learning about the weather, national airspace, aircraft systems, aerodynamics, and maneuvers. Muscle memory (re-wiring your brain) comes into play because you have to develop the fine motor skills necessary not just for taking off and landing, but for being able to fly various maneuvers while handling the radios and navigation—all at the same time. Statistics show that many people that start the training never actually finish. The challenge of getting through the initial stages of the training proves too overwhelming for many people, and they lose their commitment to go through the entire process. Some of the tricks I use to keep people motivated and committed are very much in keeping with the techniques I've described here in this book—and they work! I encourage my students to surround themselves with positive reminders of their goal; getting their license to fly. I suggest they place pictures of airplanes up on their mirrors, refrigerators, and around their computer monitors at work. I also have them sit in the airplane (on the ground!) visualizing the various elements of the maneuvers, as well as their takeoffs and landings. These activities combine goal setting, visualization and positive affirmations that they will succeed, and so far I have never had a student of mine fail a check ride! Of course, I've also been blessed with many talented students!

Goals can help us to focus our internal energy, but we also need to surround ourselves with positive people that support us and quite literally *contribute* to our energy in a healthy way. The energy that you project (negative or positive) will help bring meaningful people into your life and can also serve as a catalyst for events that may occur and push us in the right direction. We draw people into our lives that are attracted to our energy. It's a natural attractive force that exists throughout the entire universe. If your energy is positive, you will see yourself in a positive light and will likely attract the same kind of people into your life. If you are down on yourself, have low self-esteem or see yourself in a negative way, then that is exactly the kind of people you will tend to attract.

Think about this: you will either be lifted up to greater levels, buoyed by positive energy, or you will be spiraling downward in a stream of negative energy enabled by negative people or events occurring in your life. The choice is yours. The good news is that you can change the direction and flow of this energy at any time, and you will begin to see results almost immediately. When you're excited, people around you can sense your excitement, and they in turn get excited! High energy, positive attitudes are contagious. Similarly, when you are feeling negative, sad or depressed, people around you will tend to reflect this same energy. Have you ever noticed how your own moods are influenced by others?

Our lives are a journey. We are faced with choices every day, choices that can alter or change the course of our lives. It's interesting that some people seem to struggle every step of the way, besieged by "bad luck" while others seem blessed—accomplishing whatever they set out to do. We all know people like this—those that easily overcome every obstacle or hurdle thrown their way. When faced with adversity or challenges they just push through and move on. These people exude a positive energy that we can almost feel when we are close to them and they seem to always be happy, upbeat, and positive. Naturally, we all love to be around people like this because their energy and enthusiasm really *is* contagious.

Most of these people have arrived at their level of positive energy as the result of significant soul searching. Perhaps they have attained a degree of enlightenment by overcoming personal tragedy, or gained wisdom through years of living. Some have been blessed at an early age with a charm and charisma that allows them to move easily through life, surrounded by success at whatever they attempt. Regardless of how they got there—these people have discovered the *source* of their influence over other people and over their physical reality. They have mastered the power of their positive attitude... their *energy!* They exemplify the power of positive thinking and success at channeling their energy in many ways.

So how do we master our own energy force, and become that charismatic goal achiever? The process starts with a change in your attitude: Be positive and the world around you will begin to change; it will mirror your energy and respond in kind.

People you meet, events that occur in your life, adversity and challenges you are faced with are all opportunities for you to learn more about yourself, to change and improve your life. When you choose to see a challenging situation as an opportunity rather than as an obstacle, you are completely shifting your energy. By adopting a positive attitude, regardless of the circumstances or situation, you will actually change your brain chemistry, change the endorphin levels in your blood, and increase the level of serotonin in your brain. These chemical changes all lead to higher energy and heightened levels of happiness, confidence, and ultimately to greater success. The energy you project influences events, occurrences, and the people you bring into your life. Pay attention to the coincidences in your life—they are often quite meaningful. If you open your mind and listen to your inner voice you will move more easily through challenges and adversities when they do occur in your life. Something interesting happens to your brain chemistry when you're focused on a goal, and as a result, the field of energy you create around yourself changes. It's a positive change!

Once we set a goal, establish a priority, or are working positively to overcome a challenge, we are changing the *frequency* of our energy. We are resetting the vibrational levels of our internal energy to align with our attitudes and intentions. This energy is projected outward, reaching out to attract like frequencies of similar energy in the world around us. Basically, each of us vibrates with a certain frequency of energy. All matter (both organic and inorganic) all around us also vibrates at certain frequencies. This matter is made up of molecules and atoms, which on a deeper level are constructed of subatomic particles; neutrons, electrons and protons. If we peer even deeper into these subatomic particles we find that they are really not particles at all, but rather small energy bundles, held together by incredibly strong forces. These subatomic particles resonate at very specific frequencies. What exactly does this have to do with goals and challenges? Well, when we set our minds on a goal, we are establishing in our consciousness an attitude or intention that changes our brain chemistry at the subatomic level, which directly changes the frequency of the energy we project.

When we are focused on something intently, millions of neurons in our brain become *synchronized*, vibrating together much like two strings on a guitar playing the same note. These neurons, all firing together, create an electrical network in our brain that resonates at a specific frequency. This electrical energy in turn, creates an electromagnetic field that is projected outward into our physical reality—the world around us… this has been proven scientifically, and this field of energy can actually be measured and monitored. This sounds a bit technical, but all of this vibration and energy is created and projected all of the time, and very often we are completely unaware of it. *Think of it like this; each of us is a lot like a miniature radio transmitter station—we are each broadcasting our own music, and our music is based on our thoughts and intentions.* People who play "similar music" will automatically be drawn to you, and conversely you to them. The energy field that we project is based on the frequency of our attitudes and intentions embodied in our consciousness! If we desire something strongly enough we can focus our minds and channel this energy within our bodies, effectively directing this energy as we desire. When we focus our minds on *positive* thoughts, attitudes, and intentions, we alter our consciousness, and by doing so we literally alter the frequency of energy we project. By learning to focus this energy we can learn to heal our own bodies, change our physical reality, and we can move our lives in a direction of our choosing. It's all about simply being *positive.*

Whatever you do, don't let yourself get stuck in a negative "rut." You probably know, or have known someone like this at some point in time. They seem to stumble through life bouncing from job to job, relationship to relationship, or seem to be beset with just plain "bad luck" where something negative always seems to be happening. This occurs in part because they aren't listening or seeing the messages in the world around them, or taking responsibility for their own negative thoughts, energy or behavior. Negative events and situations are naturally drawn to the negative attitudes and the energy that we are projecting.

When you feel like your life isn't going well, or that the people around you always seem to be negative, or in a bad mood—take a close look at yourself and evaluate your own attitudes objectively. Is the world around you just mirroring the energy, the attitudes that you are projecting? If so, change them! If you go through life with a chip on your shoulder, more negativity is just around the corner!

Sometimes life throws us a curveball that just catches us by surprise. Have faith in yourself and those closest to you. You can get through the challenge, whatever it may be. Even when things seem to be going perfectly, there are bound to be bumps in the road along your journey. The choice about how you will deal with the setback is yours to make. Be positive, change your attitude, and view the setback or challenge as an opportunity to grow personally. You will very likely become a better person as a result of it. If there is negative energy in your life, separate yourself from it as best you can. If it is another person in your life that is projecting negative energy, get away from that person if you can and stop the negative flow. Take a few moments and consider some of the key people in your life. Are you supporting and inspiring each other? Are you lifting each other up with positive energy, or are you dragging each other down with negativity? Remember—energy flow goes both ways!

We can choose to interpret the world and respond to what life brings us in either a positive or a negative way. In my life, my own family members have taught me so much about this very thing. My younger brother Greg, for example, could easily have chosen to see the world as a negative place. His life was, in many ways, ripped apart when he was just eleven years old. Not only by the family tragedies I explained earlier, but by a series of events that upset his life following the car accident. He was forced to grow up, in large part on his own; with parents that (despite their best efforts) spent the better part of several years shuttling back and forth between work and the hospital, and then spending nearly every waking minute taking care of my sister once she came home from the hospital. As his older brother I wasn't really there for him either, I was in my own world. But instead of complaining or looking at the world in a negative way, he chose to see the good in every situation, and in the world around him. He chose to accept those accidents as challenges thrown his way and he used them as motivation to become the best person that he could. He was incredibly compassionate even at a very young age, and was instrumental in helping all of us get through the weeks and years of rehabilitation. Even as an adult he has remained exceptionally positive and caring—and he continues to see the good in every situation!

When you're faced with adversity or challenges, don't dwell on the negative but look for the positive. Be the best person that you can be, and remain positive about the cards life has dealt you, no matter how bad the outcome may seem. If you remain positive then you will surely be in a better place, attracting positive energy into your life. If you're negative, you will attract a string of negative events into your life that will certainly make things even more difficult and challenging. You have it within your power to turn a bad situation into a positive one. Make a conscious decision to live in a positive way, and surround yourself with positive people that inspire you and boost your energy. Think about it, we all naturally gravitate towards people that present an energetic positive attitude—and positive energy is contagious! Your positive attitude will create for you a happier, more balanced and fulfilling life. If you are faced with a major life challenge of your own, stay positive, never give up hope.

My sister Naomi was another shining example of handling adversity with grace. Her journey was a long one and it took a lot of hard work and commitment on her part. Remaining immobile for almost a year lying in a hospital bed had devastating effects on her muscles and her body. She had to re-learn virtually everything. We brought her home as soon as we could, my parents believed that we could provide better rehabilitation and care for her there than if she stayed in the hospital. My sister required round the clock care, and it was a hard time for all of us emotionally, but we pulled together as a family. We were grateful to have her home.

It took years of physical therapy and rehabilitation, but Naomi was determined, and over time she was able to regain some of her speech and movement. She remained confined to a wheelchair but she was completely aware mentally. Her injury was to her brain and her brain stem; the junction between the brain and the spinal cord where all the electrical messages to the central nervous system are routed, and as a result of this damage her body did not respond to her brain's signals. She spent years working with physical therapists and volunteers retraining and rewiring her brain around the injured areas in order to regain partial use and function of her limbs, as well as speech, eating and even swallowing. The human brain is *amazing*, capable of being rewired to bypass damaged areas or compensating for sensory losses with enhancement of other senses. Throughout her entire life, in spite of all that she had to deal with, Naomi always remained positive and kept her sense of humor. She lived with purpose and she was an inspiration to her family and friends. She was courageous, handled her handicaps with dignity; and was a reminder to everyone around her that *we* are the ones who decide how to live our lives. It is a choice dictated neither by our environment nor our circumstances, but by the decisions we make each day. Despite her challenges, she *chose* to be positive and she always projected a positive attitude… a positive energy.

To this day I struggle to find a "reason" for this tragedy, but I do know that each one of us learned something from it and grew from it in a profound way. We faced it as a family. We could have let the results of the accidents beat us down, but we chose instead to rise to the occasions and overcome whatever was thrown our way. This is not to say that we all didn't have our "down" days, but as a family we supported each other and made it through. Each one of us was forever changed. As I reflect back on the accidents, and the ordeal my family endured, now almost three decades ago, I am still inspired by the strength of my sister, cheered on by the positive attitude of my mom, and I truly admire the inner strength of my dad and brother for all they have overcome and for all that they still believe in.

Whatever you are going through in your personal life, no matter how great the magnitude of the challenge is, be positive and your life will change. Success will come. So, whatever your challenge, rise to the occasion. Recognize that you may very well be setting an example or offering a lesson for someone else as well. The attitude you maintain sets the tone for your life. Your attitude establishes the basis for how the world will respond to you. We all love to be around inspirational people, high-energy people, because they make us feel better—it's as though their energy is contagious. Guess what, it is… and so is yours.

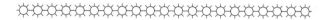

The energy we project is mirrored by the world around us. Our physical reality reacts to our energy and presents us with people or events at times when we most need support and answers. I believe that these coincidences occur at certain points in our lives to help us deal with a personal tragedy, reach a personal goal, or overcome some adversity or challenge thrown in our path. Try to remain open to the synchronicity in your own life because these coincidences will often provide you with direction on your own journey. I have experienced these coincidences so many times throughout my life that I am no longer surprised or baffled when they occur. I believe that the people I meet and events that occur in my life are progressively pushing me somewhere, and my journey continues. Every single person I meet has something to teach me, some input that can potentially change the direction of my life forever…. I try to learn from them all.

As a human race we have a natural desire to understand the bigger picture. We want to feel that our lives have purpose and meaning, we want to know who we really are and why we are here. For me, these questions became paramount in my mind, at a relatively young age. I had survived not just one, but two devastating injuries—WHY? Why had I been given not just a second chance, but a third? There must be some reason. I have spent more than three decades searching for my own answers, searching for my own truth. I've shared a bit of my own life story with you so far, and have exposed a few of the events that were life altering for me personally. I hope that in my story you have seen yourself and recognized the power of the energy that is also within *you*. I hope that this story has empowered you in some way and perhaps shown you the value of the teachers that are already present in your own life… and those you have yet to meet.

In the chapters that follow I'll provide you with the information that I have gathered over the years in my own quest for answers. Answers to those questions that address our relationship to the universe as well as the validation for the two miracles I experienced early on in my own journey. Is this energy that we project real? What proof is there? Can we really affect our own healing and change our physical reality simply by changing our attitudes and intentions? Where did that healing energy come from? How was I able to draw upon it and focus it where it was needed? How do we influence the people around us with our own energy, with our attitudes and intentions? Do we really project an energy field that serves as a catalyst for coincidence in our lives? How do we draw people into our lives that contribute to our energy?

The truth is that *the energy is real and you can translate this energy into shaping your life in a positive way.* I have tapped into this energy continuously to change my own life, my relationships, and my physical reality. I have seen the effects of this energy change the attitudes and decisions of others time and again. You really *can* turn any obstacle into an opportunity. Be open to learning from the adversity in *your* life, be aware that your energy and the energy of those around you can help you reach your goals, overcome your challenges. Be aware that your thoughts, attitude and intentions actually establish the direction for your life. I've learned a great deal from the adversities I have faced in my life, and perhaps the most important thoughts I can pass along to you are these:

☼ *Life can change in an instant, so value each moment as though it were your last.*

☼ *Surround yourself with positive people, family and friends, openly love them and tell them often.*

☼ *You can heal your own body with your energy.*

☼ *You exist in a realm beyond just your physical form.*

☼ *Your thoughts, attitudes, and intentions establish the foundation for your internal energy and determine the energy you project as well.*

☼ *Your choices and decisions determine your path in life. You alone are accountable for them.*

☼ *Change requires action, and energy is the common denominator between your choices and your actions.*

☼ *Goals and objectives give you purpose, provide a focus for your energy, and remind you where you can go and what you can accomplish with your life.*

☼ *Meditation can help you calm your mind, focus your energy, and free you from your physical constraints.*

☼ *Visualization is a powerful tool for creating the changes you desire.*

☼ *Coincidences happen for a reason, pay attention to the opportunities within them.*

☼ *Being Positive can change your life.*

And, last but not least…

☼ *You really can do anything you set your mind to!*

Chapter Four
We Become What We Think

Typically the biggest obstacle standing between us and our goals is ourselves. I'm sure you've heard this before, but it really does hold true. We tend to get in our own way and defeat ourselves with negative thoughts fueled by insecurity and lack of confidence. Negative energy can build up inside of us, becoming toxic to our minds, to our bodies, and to the people around us, virtually guaranteeing our failure. These negative thoughts can easily consume our consciousness, and as a result translate into the energy we project. This negative energy can serve as the foundation of our projected electromagnetic field just as readily as positive energy can. Ultimately, the choice of which type of energy we project is up to us.

The world mirrors the energy that we project and does not filter or differentiate between the positive or negative energy. Dr. Masaru Emoto illustrates this beautifully in his book, *Love Thyself The Messages From Water III*. His research and findings offer factual and photographic evidence which clearly demonstrate the physical response of water to the projection of human vibrational energy, thoughts, and words. His work also shows the effect of different environmental conditions (such as pollution) on the molecular structure of water as it freezes, and even demonstrates the impact of different types of music on water molecules. It is interesting to note from his research that "positive energy" (in its various forms, such as love) always seemed to "create beautiful crystalline images within the water molecules and negative energy typically created ugly, distorted shapes, colors and patterns!"[1] His fascinating experiments are well documented and seem to conclusively demonstrate the vibrational interaction of our thoughts and emotions on elements of our physical reality.

Most of us can also relate to this "projecting" of energy within our own personal relationships, albeit in a slightly different manner. Say, for example, that you come home from work in a terrible mood—your boss yelled at you, your project deadline came and went because your color printer broke, and you still have hours of work to do to prepare for tomorrow's presentation. You walk in the door to a happy wife, kids who want to tell you all about their day at school, and the dog wagging his tail… but within minutes of entering the room you can sense a change in the air. The dog goes to the corner and lies down, the kids quietly disappear to their rooms, and your wife's smile disappears. Everyone, including the dog, has sensed your negative energy and responded to it instantly. Does this sound at all familiar? Our attitudes and intentions are mirrored in the people and events that occur around us. In the case of negative energy, we can be surrounded by people that add to our grief, create barriers to our happiness, and become a catalyst for events that increase the negative energy in our environment. To counteract this negative energy and its inherent issues, you must change your perspective, change your attitudes, and develop positive intentions towards the people you interact with and the world around you. By doing so, you will change your life. I know this seems almost ridiculously simple; but it really *does* work. Our attitudes and our intentions change the frequency of the energy we project, and the world around us will *always* mirror this energy.

Achieving a balance between your internal energy and your external environment opens a conduit: an energy pipeline between your consciousness and your physical reality. For example, the balance between mind and body achieved through physical exercise adds tremendously to the free flow of energy within your body, and it also adds to the calming effects it can have on your overall sense of well being. When you exercise you are not only releasing stress and burning out toxins in your blood, but also increasing your overall level of serotonin, the "happy chemical" in your brain, all of which contributes to the improvement of your overall physical health. An "open pipeline" encourages the smooth flow of energy within your mind, throughout your body, and outward into your physical reality—literally connecting you to the universe itself. If the energy flows openly, you can wash away the unwanted, negative energy, replacing it with positive energy instead. Each of us has a unique internal rhythm of energy that flows throughout our bodies; we each vibrate at a unique set of frequencies. Your frequency of energy is always directly tuned to your attitude and intentions. It is important for you to look closely at yourself, your thoughts, habits and beliefs in order to discover your own internal rhythms and cycles. If you do your best thinking in the morning—then schedule your day accordingly. If you find that there are certain activities that help you feel balanced or bring you joy, like running or gardening, or hiking—then be sure to make time for those things in your schedule. Don't forget to honor your own needs, your natural rhythm and internal cycles. This is important for maintaining a healthy balance in your life.

When we resist our internal flow of energy, or do things that don't feel right for us—we automatically fall out of balance, out of harmony with ourselves and the world around us. If we are out of balance with our *own* energy then we will definitely be out of balance with the frequency of the energy in nature and the world around us! An imbalance of energy will only make it more difficult for us to focus, and therefore far more challenging for us to achieve our goals, whatever they may be. Here's an example of what I mean. When you do something that doesn't feel right, something that you know is wrong or could possibly hurt someone else, this instantly creates a feeling of guilt in your subconscious. This negative emotion will eat at you from the inside; subtly destroying your energy and self esteem, and it can even build up to a more toxic level making you angry and caustic. This negative internal energy can also potentially manifest itself by making you physically ill. So, make decisions in your life that will make you feel good about yourself. An unbalanced life allows negative energy to creep in and influence your attitude and intentions. If you need to hit the gym every morning for an hour before you go to work to keep your energy level balanced, then make it a priority and do just that!

Is it natural or realistic for us to walk around all day with a bright smile on our faces, and nothing but sugar plum fairies and happy endings to brighten our moods? Of course not, nature has its cycles. Life has its ups and downs. Negative energy and positive energy are part of our natural cycle. We can't be positive all of the time, and it's perfectly normal to have down cycles, bad moods, and negative energy in our systems occasionally. If we can learn to accept some of the negative aspects of our lives, the negative energy, as a part of our natural cycle, then we can learn to not *dwell* in the negative, but rather to simply see it for what it is, deal with it, and move through it, keeping our focus on the positive. We have to learn to handle the negative cycles, stay balanced, and increase our positive energy. *We just have to minimize the negative and maximize the positive!* We can accomplish this by keeping our thoughts positive, in addition to our attitudes about ourselves and our perspective on everything around us. Remember, we can choose to see either the positive or the negative in *everything* that occurs in our lives... it's a choice we make! We become what we think, and the world around us mirrors our attitudes and beliefs about ourselves.

So, how do we increase our bias towards the positive? For me personally, I find that setting and achieving goals and objectives in both my personal and professional life works. Setting clear goals keeps me focused and when I achieve my objectives (whether large or small) I always feel a sense of pride and accomplishment. This, in turn, makes me feel valuable and happy! I also try to keep myself surrounded by positive people as much as I can, and I use affirmations on a regular basis. Affirmations are positive statements regarding changes we want to make, or goals and objectives we wish to achieve. They are another great way to help us maintain a belief in ourselves and in the direction we are moving, and they also help us to stay focused on our goals and objectives—on those positive changes we want to make in our lives. When written down (affirmations become stronger and more "real" when we write them down), looked at and verbalized frequently, they keep our minds focused and our intentions clear and specific in relation to those very objectives. They work to keep the energy of our minds tuned to the proper frequency, leading to an enhanced focus of our positive energy and ultimately to the outcome we wish to achieve.

Our conscious and subconscious minds play important roles in tuning the frequency of the energy patterns that we project. Our actions are indicative of our deepest feelings, our thoughts and emotions, even those that we may be unaware of. This is because our bodies possess a tremendous electrical energy, rooted in the very molecules and atoms that make up all of our tissues, bones, and organs. In fact, this energy (stored in the form of electrochemical energy) is used not only to fuel our muscles and organs, but it also serves as the stimulus of electrical energy through our entire central nervous system; from our brains right down to our toes. This energy fuels and affects every function of every vital organ, the movement of our muscles, and even our thoughts and memories. This is the same electrical energy that crosses the synapses (the small gaps that span all of the billions of neurons in our brain) creating a network of energy that contains all of our memories and thoughts. It is really not that different from the electrical energy that powers our IPods, or our cell phones.

Here's how it works. Our brains are a huge complex network of brain cells (neurons) that are all interconnected via those synapses. These neurons in our brain are continuously creating various chemical reactions in response to our attitudes and thoughts. These chemical reactions result in the creation of a very small amount of electrical energy that is transmitted across the synapses of adjoining neurons. When we remember something—a treasured childhood memory perhaps, these connected neurons are sending information to one another across the synapses, sometimes in very different parts of our brains. The chemical reactions that occur vary depending upon the specific activity or thought; and the frequency and strength of the energy that is being created changes as our thoughts change. When all of these neurons in our brains are firing, the connections across neurons create an electrical network, and the very essence of our thoughts and memories is stored in this vast network. Changing your attitudes, thoughts and intentions changes the frequency of energy you project, just like changing the station on your radio.

Typically in life, much of what we do is on autopilot… we are not always completely focused on the task at hand. We might be working on one thing, but subconsciously contemplating several others at the same time. Our brains handle this just fine, but in situations like this we are not really utilizing our potential. In order to use our minds to their fullest potential and strengthen our energy fields, we want to *increase* the flow of internal energy. *This increase happens when there are millions of our neurons firing in synchronicity across both the left and right hemispheres of our brains.* This synchronous firing and increased flow of energy readily occurs during meditation or during those periods of time when we are intensely focused on something. In these moments our brain actually creates a *stronger* electromagnetic field—with a frequency dictated by our thoughts, feelings, and intentions. So, we can learn to *strengthen* our energy projection and *enhance* our abilities to affect change in our external (and internal) realities by focusing our thoughts and maintaining balance in our lives. In this manner, we quite literally become more powerful. Our energy fields are constantly projected outward, transmitting our intentions to the world around us, and seeking to align with similar energy —that of other people and of our physical reality.

In his paper, "Evidence of an Electromagnetic Field Theory of Consciousness," Dr. Johnjoe McFadden cites a variety of analysis and clinical studies in which EEG signals from study participants have been measured in various states of mental activity—including: sleep and REM dreaming, comatose states of patients, and active problem solving. His research provides validation that the "dynamic complexity (of the EEG patterns) is increased during creative thinking but decreased during coma or deep sleep, raised during REM dreaming, and… markedly affected during conscious thinking, and even changed while listening to music, indicating the route by which music may influence the complexity of our conscious thought patterns."[2] Therefore, whatever activity or thought process you are involved in changes both your energy field *and* the strength of its projection, and this happens even when you are unconscious… you are projecting your energy outward twenty-four hours a day!

Ancient Eastern Mystics have described an enlightened state of being or consciousness as the state of mind that occurs when we are *tuned with our own internal energy frequencies and in tune with that of nature around us.* This concept of "tuning" refers to the synchronization of the frequency of energy we project. Through deep meditation we are able to quiet the noise of our external world and achieve a state of consciousness where our physical reality disappears leaving us free to explore our own internal feelings and thoughts. Their general belief is that true enlightenment can only occur when we become one with ourselves and with nature… when we are in complete synchronicity and at peace with ourselves and with the universe.

Life is dynamic, constantly changing, constantly in flux; and so are our day-to-day lives. We evolve on a daily basis. Because of these constant changes in our lives, our thoughts and attitudes are in a dynamic state of change as well. Our lives play out as a journey from the moment we are born until the time we die, and the path we follow is continuously influenced by both our attitudes and our thoughts. We are constantly faced with decisions, and the choices we make will also influence the direction our path will take.

The alignment of your positive energy field with that of the world around you will begin to influence (with increased frequency and repetition) both people and events that will ultimately help you to reach your goals and objectives. The energy of the universe aligns with yours, and your personal thoughts and beliefs (at both the conscious *and* subconscious level) will begin to manifest exactly as you desire, strengthening both your own internal energy and your resolve to remain focused on your own path. This alignment of frequencies, between you and the world around you, compounds the energy from both, resulting in an additive effect which increases the energy you have available for overcoming any adversity or setback that could otherwise deter you from your primary focus.

So how do you find this inner calm that allows you to balance your energy with the world around you? How do you know if you are following a path that will allow you to reach your true potential? You can start by paying attention to your inner most thoughts and beliefs about yourself, and how you react to various situations in life. You might want to use a journal to record your observations. Notice where there is room to shift to a more positive approach, and take time to find the balance you need in your life. Make time in your schedule to do the things that really make you happy and bring a sense of inner peace. In this way you begin to align yourself and your energy with that of the world around you. I believe that we are each on a journey that spans our entire lives. Most of us want to achieve our true potential, to be of value and service to others, and to feel like we have meant something to the people we love in our lives.

In fact, one of the reasons you are probably reading this book right now, is that you are looking for answers. Please remember that your personal journey isn't just defined by the path you follow through your physical reality (your job, family, and so on) but that it is also defined by your *inward* journey—one that explores questions about who you are, how you define yourself, and why you are placed here on this Earth. We all have infinite potential. Look deep within yourself; explore your feelings, and your strengths. As you begin this inward exploration, try to perceive things intuitively—not just logically. Listen to your inner voice, your gut instincts, and hear what your mind and heart are telling you. *Listen to both the emotional and intellectual sides of your brain together.* If you can hear both your intuitive and logical voices, you will be able to discover and follow a path that is right for you.

Your simultaneous inward and outward journeys must converge in order to achieve a true balance of your energy. The idea here is not just to manifest things in your life on an external level, but to expand your internal horizons, as well. Without the inward journey, the physical reality lacks depth and meaning. Understanding yourself is vital, and through increased self-awareness you can begin to identify and resolve any internal conflicts that may be creating negative energy or causing barriers to your growth and development. Internal conflicts quite naturally arise when your life goes in a direction that's different from your expectations or desires. For example, maybe that promotion or bonus you were expecting didn't materialize, or perhaps you are experiencing unexpected financial difficulties, or you are faced with a sudden illness. Despite your best preparations, life never goes exactly as you plan! Identifying these areas of stress or tension in your life will bring them to the forefront of your awareness and allow you to resolve them more readily. Strategically focus your energy to resolve these conflicts. It's important to maintain a positive outlook on the future, and see yourself working through whatever it is you are dealing with—knowing that you can and will overcome the challenges placed before you.

Through a shift in your attitude, away from the negative aspects of your internal conflicts and toward more positive expectations, you will begin to see an immediate improvement in your outlook and find much greater insight and clarity. This clarity will facilitate the resolution of the issues in a way that is more favorable to achieving your goals. You can also change the way you perceive your conflicts; choose to see the larger picture and the broader patterns that may exist, and this may very well lead you down an entirely different path to reach your goals. You must learn to let go of your need to control in order to grow and evolve. By looking at your challenges or conflicts from a different perspective; not as barriers—but rather as opportunities— you encourage a different way of thinking within yourself, and you shift your energy field. Allow yourself to find hope—even in what may seem like a desperate situation. If you allow your mind to stay negative or clouded with panic you will never find a clear path forward.

When you choose to re-evaluate your challenges or conflicts from a different more positive perspective a couple of really interesting physiological changes occur. Your brain chemistry changes *immediately*; your endorphin levels rise and so do your serotonin levels; both of which make you feel *good*. As these chemical changes occur, your internal energy and frequency patterns will begin to harmonize. Then, tension in your body begins to melt away, the muscles in your chest relax and your breathing slows, instantly improving the balance in your blood chemistry. Your blood pressure goes down and your mind begins to clear allowing new and different thoughts to enter. These physiological changes are *real*, and they impact how you think.

When conflicts arise, or you are feeling at odds with yourself, pause for a moment, take a few deep breaths and ask yourself these questions:

What am I not happy about? Why I am I feeling agitated? What is the real source of the conflict? Allow yourself to relax, breathe more slowly, and you can systematically explore your body, your attitudes about yourself, your relationships, your career, finances, and so on, seeking the source of the conflict. Try it now… close your eyes and take two or three deep breaths and exhale slowly; feel your mind and body relax!

Once you have uncovered the source of the stress or conflict, you can then begin to shift your mindset towards resolution, towards a more positive direction that will resolve the issue or conflict. If you can view your life from a broader perspective, you will likely see beyond the problem or challenge to possible solutions. Don't waste time or energy trying to find someone to blame, regardless of the issue. Start with yourself, keep your mind and heart open and look at what you can do to resolve the challenge. From there you can move forward, looking for possible solutions. If you are dealing with conflict between yourself and another person or group, try to view the source of the conflict from their perspective, and mentally assume their role in the situation at hand. Put yourself in their shoes for a moment. Stop the flow of negative energy and open your mind to different, more positive solutions, then re-center your own energy and thoughts around this different solution or approach. Your positive energy combined with a solution that may be more palatable from their perspective will open the flow of energy and help bring everyone together, working towards an amicable resolution.

I experienced this for myself right after I had spent dozens of hours editing this book manuscript. I was diligently saving the edits on my memory stick so I could transfer them from one computer to another. I had finished a solid twelve hours a little before midnight the previous night, saved my changes and gone to bed. I got up the following morning, turned the computer on, and pulled up the manuscript with my last three days of changes incorporated. What

I had in front of me was two hundred pages of "little y's!" If you've ever lost an entire document like this; you've seen this same thing and you can relate to the complete dismay and frustration that I felt. The file had somehow been corrupted, and I had lost three days of original edits that I would never be able to duplicate. But, it was my own fault for not backing it up in several places—so this was a perfect opportunity to practice what I have been preaching. This certainly seemed like a negative event, but I had a deadline and couldn't waste time or energy dwelling on exactly how the file got corrupted, or beating myself up mentally—the only thing to do was to sit down and start editing again. Who knows, maybe the newer version of the edits was "meant to be"—perhaps it would speak to someone in a way the first version would not have, or it would communicate my messages more clearly!

How many times has this type of thing happened to you and how did you handle it? Learn to think outside of your normal constraints and be creative. Once you view everything from a broader perspective you will begin to see that there are usually multiple paths to the same goal. Depending on how big a challenge you are dealing with, it sometimes helps to get a pad of paper out and write down at the top of the page your issues, challenges, goals, dilemmas, or whatever it may be that you want to accomplish. Write down the associated conflicts or issues with each. From there jot down some possible solutions, people involved, challenges and risks, with each approach. Once you've done that—take a step back and evaluate the various solutions both from a risk and likely outcome perspective. You may very well see a different path.

Look objectively at your approaches; you might want to combine several of them, to come up with a new hybrid way to approach the problem. Chances are that you will see a myriad of possibilities you never imagined, once you open your mind up to more creative solutions and you are looking at the bigger picture. Your energy will then flow much more freely, leading you towards a solution.

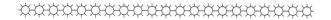

We each have the power of choice in our lives, the power to change how we think about ourselves. We also have the power to change how and what we think about the world we live in. It is completely within our reach to change ourselves and the world around us. The first and most important step is to shift our attitudes and our mindset: *Be positive!*

As human beings we have an unlimited capacity for growth, for change, and for love. Learn to accept yourself for who you are and accept other people for who they are as well. This means changing your attitudes about yourself, and also about the people around you. Don't judge others harshly—this only sets up a negative energy exchange and produces emotions that will drain your internal energy. Don't judge yourself harshly, either. Know your weaknesses, but also know your strengths, and always communicate honestly with yourself and others. Negative attitudes, low self-esteem and low self-confidence will typically just breed fear, depression, and negative energy. Harboring ill will against others or indulging in negative self-talk only diminishes your capacity for love and changes your flow of energy. If you think negative, self-effacing thoughts, then the frequency of the energy that you project will be based on negative energy and will attract similar energy from the people and world around you.

My daughter, McCall, is a student at Berkeley. She is in an Architecture degree program. She's smart, disciplined and very positive about getting through all of her degree requirements. However, during her freshman year we would get frequent "distress" calls from her; weekly, and sometimes even daily. It was obvious to us as parents that she was feeling overwhelmed, having a tough time adjusting and it seemed as though she was well on her way to a meltdown. We honestly weren't sure she was going to make it. All of the work, tough classes, "study more" attitudes from the GSI's and professors, compounded and added to her feelings of insecurity about whether or not she was as smart as the kids around her, even through her grades were well above average. It was clear to us that she was letting the negative energy in her build up, and as a result, the world around her seemed like it was falling apart. From the bad food to the problems in her dorm, her lack of sleep, and the professors drilling her to work harder, her world was mirroring her negative energy.

Over time, with our love, constant support, reinforcement (and an occasional kick in the pants) she pushed through her challenges. Her attitude changed significantly during her sophomore year; she joined a sorority, she resolved to remain positive and the world around her changed too. She pushed away the negative energy, replaced it with a positive attitude and positive energy, and she is now close to graduating with her degree near the top of her class. Our external support and positive energy helped her to work through the tough spots, too. Metaphorically speaking, she no longer looked at the huge mountain she had to climb, but instead she focused on getting to the top of each of the small foothills that made up the mountain, climbing those hills one step at a time. We would tell her on every one of those phone calls that first year, "Don't try to climb the mountain in one big step, don't even look at the mountain ahead, just look at the next few steps you need to make and take them one step at a time."

We have all experienced times in our lives where the challenges just seemed overwhelming. When this happens, take a step back and look for the progress you've made, acknowledge the positive things that you've accomplished. Remember that nature has its own cycles just like you do. You have to accept the negative cycles but push past them. Move through the negative energy, bad mood, feelings of insecurity or frustrations as quickly as possible. Focus on being positive about where you are, realize how far you've come and see the good things in your life. Understand that these cycles and challenges are normal. Keep your final goal in mind, but climb your mountain one small hill, one small step at a time; and you will certainly reach the top.

So, balance your energy, focus your thoughts on the positive and the world around you *will* change. Live compassionately, live with commitment, follow your intuition, and be your own biggest fan. Once you know yourself, and have balanced your internal energy, you will be well positioned to move forward. Strive to become increasingly aware of the world around you and make the most of every single moment. Have reverence for life, faith in humanity, and faith in your own strengths and your ability to reach your goals and overcome your challenges. A positive attitude about yourself, your surroundings, the world around you, and the people in your life will increase your endorphin levels, change your brain chemistry and the energy field you project will be a positive one. This in turn will draw more positive influences into your life because the world around you will reflect your positive energy. You become what you think.

When you have a goal worth pursuing, and you are faced with major challenges or obstacles that seem to get in the way of your success, just stick with it; stay focused and push through the challenges and obstacles. It's entirely normal to feel like giving up, or wanting to quit when the challenges seem insurmountable... and this may seem like the easier path sometimes, but don't give in to the negative energy, stay positive, visualize your success, and push through the discomfort. When you do reach your goal the sense of satisfaction and accomplishment will be tremendous. You'll soon forget the obstacles and pain you endured in the process and will soon be ready to take on new and even more challenging goals.

Vic, a coworker of mine, had always wanted to run the Los Angeles Marathon, but one major obstacle stood in his way. He was overweight, out of shape, and hadn't run more than the distance from his couch to the refrigerator for a beer during the halftime show for the past few years. He was, however, committed and wanted to accomplish this as a personal life goal. So he started slowly. He didn't look at running the whole twenty-six miles, he started by first running around the block, and then he gradually worked his way up to five miles a week, and upwards from there. He had pictures of runners blowing through the finish line taped all over his office. He visualized his success. He ran into a few training plateaus along the way, but stuck with his diet and his running regime. Race day rolled around and he was ready. Starting out towards the middle of the pack, Vic was both anxious and excited at the same time. The starting gun went off and away he went. He pushed through the pain—reaching the ten mile point, pushed through the mind trickery that occurs at twenty miles, and willed his body through the last two miles to the finish line! You see, he shifted his energy, pushed through the challenges along the way, stuck with it, and achieved his life goal—and so can you. *Set goals, visualize your own success and push through your challenges to achieve your own personal objectives.*

To accomplish the goals in your life or overcome major challenges you may be faced with, whatever they may be, you must first find the energy and motivation within yourself to overcome your challenges, to meet your personal goals. Don't look for someone else to solve your problems or to make things happen for you. It's a lot like trying to get your kids to study or do their homework. You can encourage and cajole them into sitting down, and getting it done, but this only works for a short while, probably only through Elementary school. Ultimately, they've got to find their own internal motivation to study and get good grades. You can't do the work for them; they have to learn self-discipline, do it themselves and take pride in their work. As they get older and become more independent it becomes even more apparent that the external motivation from their parents is not enough. If they haven't developed their own discipline or self-motivation by high school, the results will be obvious. Much like life, school grades will deliver exactly the results of their efforts. While they may be able to get away with this for a while in junior high or high school, by the time they get to college they will quickly discover, that in order to be successful, their commitment and motivation has to come from within. Ultimately, your commitment must come from within as well.

Success is hard work, make no mistake about it. It takes action on your part to achieve it. Wake up every day and work hard at being successful, meeting your challenges, and overcoming your adversity. You possess an energy that manifests in your thoughts, attitudes and intentions, so keep it positive. You continually project this energy outward and it ripples throughout the world around you, aligning to bring you the success you desire.

We've talked a lot about the psychology behind positive attitudes and energy, and a little bit about the science behind the energy within each of us. To be frank it is impossible to completely separate the psychological explanations from the scientific ones. As human beings we have free will and our thoughts, attitudes and choices are critical components of how our energy interacts with the world around us. We will get into further detail about the mechanics of how this energy works later in this book, but for now—just remember that the energy we have been discussing is *real*.

Major discoveries in quantum physics have come as a result of looking deeper into the subatomic realm. We have learned, in just the past few decades, that atoms which are the building blocks of all matter, are *not* made up of smaller particles (like we first learned about in junior high science class) but that they are really made up of *very small energy bundles*. These energy bundles (the electron, proton and neutron particles) vibrate at specific frequencies, much like the string on a guitar vibrates when you pluck it. Only in recent years have technology and science advanced to a point where we have been able to begin an exploration deep into this subatomic realm. Here scientists have found many answers, and raised just as many new questions. *The more deeply we look within the structure of the atom, the more we discover that it is all energy; vibrating energy that is interconnected to all other energy across the universe.*

This is an important point: The atoms—which make up all matter that exists—are comprised of energy bundles that vibrate or resonate at specific frequencies. Each of us is really a mass of vibrating energy, and all this energy is connected throughout the universe! Think about this for a moment…

❖ Everything around us is energy.

❖ Everything inside of us is energy; literally, all matter is energy.

❖ We are the essence of energy—vibrating at a specific frequency.

❖ All energy is interconnected across the entire universe.

❖ We are connected to all energy throughout the universe!

The laws of nature favor a balance of this energy and resist imbalance. Nature itself renews and rebalances its own forces through cycles such as; day and night, the seasons, the weather, and even life and death for all living creatures. We know that the very basic elements of all matter and energy, are created and destroyed in a continuous, spontaneous cycle. The universe is an entity comprised of integrated components, which individually and together acknowledge this balance of cycles in nature. We'll discuss the importance of balance in our lives further in chapter eight, but for now, know that just as nature balances itself; we too must seek balance. You are probably familiar with the concept of Yin and Yang, which is described as a balance of the forces in nature. The Taoists describe the balancing of this energy as an active process between the yielding/passive and active/dynamic energy.

We all learned Albert Einstein's theory of relativity back in our high school science classes; the famous E=MC2, which is: Energy (E) equals Mass (M) times the speed of light squared (C2). What Einstein's theory basically tells us is that all matter is indeed energy. Simply put, it states that the mass of a body is a measure of its *energy* content. Even the mass of a chair or a rock has stored energy! Most of us have no idea just how powerful we really are... to put this into perspective: The energy stored in the atoms and molecules in each one of us as individuals, if released all at one time, would be roughly the equivalent of the energy in five (50 kiloton) atomic bombs!

So, each of us *and* everything in our physical reality is made up of these vibrating energy bundles, they are all around us, and inside of us, too. I know it's hard to grasp the fact that what we see or perceive as a solid matter isn't solid at all, but actually just a complex network of molecules, atoms and smaller particles (which are really just energy bundles) all vibrating at specific frequencies. This frequency is the basis for the energy that all matter possesses, and this energy is real! The frequency of energy is the foundation for all phenomena we detect with our senses; from other people and from our immediate physical reality. The faster these energy bundles vibrate the less likely we will be able to "sense" them with our five senses, but when this vibrational energy is constrained in a small space, like the structure of the atoms and molecules that make up this book in your hands, the easier it is for us to sense the energy... to touch it, see it, smell it, hear it or taste it. It is only when we operate on a level beyond our five senses that we can sense the "unconstrained" vibrational energy moving at the higher, faster frequencies, but we'll address that subject in greater depth later on.

Suffice it to say for now, that energy always responds to the frequency of similar energy through the mutual attraction laws of nature. On a large scale, gravity works this way—like the attractive forces between the Earth and the moon, and on a small scale— it's these same forces that hold the particles of the atom together. Specific frequencies of energy attract other similar frequencies of energy. This fact is the very basis for many of the coincidences and synchronicity in our life's—and this energy is also the basis for the miraculous healing powers that we each possess.

✧✧✧✧✧✧✧✧✧✧✧✧✧✧✧✧✧✧✧✧✧

We can heal our own bodies, become what we think, change the world around us. How does this work? The frequencies of energy that are developed in each of our brains can actually be measured. Remember, we can change the frequency of the electrical patterns within our brains at will by changing our thoughts, attitudes, and intentions. You may recall the use of simple electroencephalography (EEG) testing used back in the day before MRI's and Cat Scans. These EEG tests were nothing more than measuring the electrical output of the brains activity. The doctors were able to diagnose problems in the brain based on the mapping of the electromagnetic output of your brain waves. EEG testing is now considered fairly primitive by today's standards but it is a recognizable means of measuring energy fields that we are all relatively familiar with.

Here's an example of just how the brain can be transformed "electrically" through meditation, not only to produce short term relaxation and feelings of happiness, but also to produce permanent "wiring changes" within the network connections of neurons in our brains, ultimately strengthening the energy field that we project. Some fascinating research was done by Dr. Richard Davidson, a neuroscientist at the W.M. Keck Laboratory for Functional Brain Imaging, that involved Tibet's Dalai Lama and eight of his most accomplished meditation practitioners.

His study involved this particular group of Tibetan monks who were extremely well versed in meditation along with a control group of students. They were all connected to EEG machines and asked to meditate, with their focus on "unconditional compassion" for various periods of time. Dr. Davidson was specifically looking to validate the "gamma wave," which is created by the high frequency output of the brains electrical activity during these periods of calming meditation. Davidson said that the results (of his research) clearly showed that meditation activated the trained minds of the monks in *significantly* different ways from the group of untrained student volunteers. Most importantly, the electrodes (the EEG) picked up much greater activation of fast moving and unusually powerful gamma waves in the monks. The movement of the waves (as measured by the EEG's) through the brains of the monks was far better organized and coordinated than that of the students. His research went on to show the mental activities such as focus, memory, learning, and consciousness are all associated with the kind of "superior neural coordination" found in the monks. The intense gamma waves they produced have also been subsequently linked to the knitting together of "disparate brain circuits" that allowed higher mental activity, heightened awareness, and increased physiological functioning. The monks had been successful at re-wiring their brains through continued positive thoughts that resulted from years of discipline and meditation. The students who served as a control group also showed marked improvements during the course of the experiment. This particular study serves to confirm that the efficacy and healing powers of the brain can be significantly enhanced through the regular practice of deep meditation.[3]

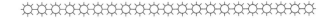

We as human beings are basically a large network of living energy that is vibrating at specific frequencies. All of the cells in our body are continuously going through their own renewal cycles—much like nature does on a far grander scale. All of this energy; the energy that is within each one of the cells in our bodies and that of all other matter, is inextricably linked through common forces that bind these subatomic particles together. Moreover, the energy that exists across the universe is connected, and life energy reaches out across the universe in search of *similar* life energy. On a broader scale, this energy and the forces behind this energy, connects all matter that exists across the universe—and every bit of it can be linked back to the "Big Bang" Theory, [4] the event that led to the creation of the universe, all matter that exists within it, and the beginning of space-time!

Not only can we tie the science and psychology together, but we also can tie this information to spiritual and religious beliefs throughout the ages. We have seen a unique convergence between recent scientific discoveries and the text and teachings of many ancient Eastern religious philosophies dating back to more than twenty-five hundred years ago. Ancient philosophers conclude that an ultimate energy lies at the core of all matter that exists and that this energy is all connected through nature, a conclusion that is remarkably similar to the conclusions of physicists today. Scientists and philosophers both allude to the existence of a supreme, divine energy, an energy that many of the world's religions refer to as God. Physicists hope to soon uncover what they believe to be the ultimate source of this energy, the core energy particle described as the Higgs Boson, which has at this time been theorized, but not yet discovered. [5]

This universal energy we have been discussing is science *fact*—not science fiction. It exists deep within the energy bundles that make up each atom at the cellular level throughout our bodies; it's generated electrochemically within the neurons in our brain. It exists in *everything* all around you right now; it even makes up the atoms in the paper of this book. This same energy pulses and flows throughout our veins and in our blood, and surges throughout our central nervous system carrying the signals that direct our organs and muscles. When we are in a calm, balanced state of mind, focused and intent on some process of thought—millions of these neurons are firing synchronously. Many studies have been done which have established the basis for theories showing that our consciousness is embodied in an electromagnetic field—generated by this massive number of synchronous neurons firing in our brain. Dr. McFadden called his theory "the CEMI theory."[2] In essence it states that this electromagnetic force (the energy generated by these millions of neurons firing together) is naturally projected outward into the immediate region surrounding our bodies. This projection of energy, moving outward at specific frequencies, is the positive or negative energy that is generated directly by our thoughts, our attitudes and our intentions. This energy synchronizes with the energy fields around us and serves to directly link us, our actions, desires, attitudes and intentions with similar energy in our physical reality. Carl Jung postulated that this is the energy force which "motivates coincidences and synchronicities in our lives to occur."[6] This is the same energy that we can learn to control through our thoughts, attitudes and intentions and by harnessing it we can affect the changes and transformations in our lives that we desire. This energy, and more specifically the frequency of this energy, can heal our bodies, change our physical reality, and change our lives.

Why is this concept important? This process of energy transformation and change begins within us. By finding a balance of our internal energy, centered on positive elements of our lives, and ourselves, we find a deep source of unlimited energy, an inner peace, and a tranquility that strengthens and balances our own internal energy field allowing us to interact more powerfully with the world around us. Many ancient prophets and Eastern Mystics found their balance of energy through a lifetime of meditation. During the healing phases of my own injuries, I too, found and tapped into this vast resource of internal and external energy all around me through meditation. While I personally feel this is probably one of the best methods for tapping into our own energy resources, there are certainly many other techniques we can use as well. Simple focus, breathing and self-calming techniques are just a few. Combined with changes in our thought patterns, intentions and attitudes, they will all provide an excellent springboard from which to begin the process of change.

The world around us is constantly evolving, continuously going through its own process of life, death, and renewal; just like the cells in our bodies are; just like we are. The subatomic particles that make up all atoms, in all matter, similarly go through a renewal cycle of spontaneous degeneration and regeneration. Nature is ever changing, constantly in motion, very much like the cyclical energy that moves through the universe. As human beings, we are also a complex network of this same energy; so it is only natural that our lives are in constant motion. It's important to embrace change, embrace this motion as a natural function of life.

Whether you change your life through the power of prayer and belief in a supreme being, or change your life through meditation or even psychotherapy, you are still making a change in your attitude and intentions. It doesn't matter so much *how* you get there—just that you *do* get there. Do what feels right for you. The changes in your attitude and intentions will alter and change the pattern of energy in your brain along with your brain chemistry—changing the pattern of energy that you project. By changing your attitude and intentions, and creating a more positive projection of your internal energy, the people and world around you will respond accordingly.

Change is an active process. Certainly, the process of change can begin with a change in your attitude, and it could even be inspired by knowledge or insight that you may have gained by reading this book, but reading this book or any other book is not enough. In order to effect lasting change in your life you must take action. Action requires a goal, it requires sustained and lasting change in your attitude, a plan, schedule, and most importantly: action relative to your plan. An activity that is repeated often enough, beginning with small steps, integrated over time, will lead you to success. Take action to change your life starting now.

Don't resist or fear change. If you feel stuck in a bad job, a bad relationship, poor economic conditions, or ill health; don't run from the situation—face it head on and embrace this opportunity for change as part of a natural cycle. You have the power to change the negative things in your life; you have the power of choice. Begin the change with yourself, with your attitudes, own your energy. If you've made some mistakes, accept them, learn from them and move on. Living in an internal or external environment that is negative only breeds more negative energy. Make the choice now to change your attitudes and your world will begin to reflect the new attitude and positive energy that you project.

Life doesn't treat you in any particular way, good or bad. In fact, it isn't really "life treating you," it's the world "responding to you"—responding to the energy field that you project. Luck, in my opinion, has really very little to do with the outcome of your life. We get out of life what we cultivate. As I mentioned earlier, the world and people around us mirror the energy we project. The Ancient Eastern Mystics, the Buddhists, Hindus, and the Taoists—in their collective wisdom, all concur that our physical reality reflects our inner energy. If you think life is pretty good, and you feel good about the direction that your life is going—

then you will project this positive attitude and the world around you will mirror the energy you project. The quality of your life will improve, just as you expect it to. Similarly, if you think that the world is treating you poorly, and bad luck seems to follow your every step, then the negative energy that you project is again being reflected by the world around you. You become what you believe in, and you are what you think. This is why a positive attitude is so important. Your attitude and intentions are very powerful forces in your life. Your life is as you intend it to be.

Cultivate positive energy in your life and you will discover that your internal energy will begin to build upon itself. Surround yourself with positive, high energy people and your energy will increase even further. Distance yourself from negative people, negative energy and attitudes because they will only drain you of your positive energy. Reflect daily on the good things in your life, those things that bring you satisfaction and joy. Reflect on your goals and objectives, re-assess your challenges from a broad perspective; re-affirm your commitment to overcome adversity, and to successfully reach your goals. Do your best to remain positive about yourself and your life!

By learning to focus and harness your internal energy you will be able to not only improve the quality of your own life but to improve the quality of the lives of the people around you. The people you are closest with, both family and friends will see the changes in you. You will discover that your overall health and sense of well being improves as your positive energy builds. You will find that your influence with those around you begins to increase. People are naturally drawn to others that have a positive attitude and high energy. Your outward projection of positive energy, the frequency of your energy becomes increasingly synchronized internally, and with your external world. Coincidences, events, and people that can help you reach your goals, or overcome your personal challenges, will increasingly become a part of your life, and you will start to become more aware of their importance as they occur. Stay open to this synchronicity in your life and pay attention to the messages or information that may be inherent within an occurrence or event. These "coincidences" are really meaningful opportunities that result directly from the outward projection of your energy field and thus occur specifically because of your intentions.

Exactly how does this energy get projected outward? Think of it this way. If you throw a rock into a calm lake—the impact of the rock with the water will create circular waves that project outward. This is exactly what your positive attitude and intentions do. The energy created by your thoughts and intentions is like that rock you tossed into the lake. This energy establishes an electromagnetic field that ripples out into the world around you. Consider that the more focused your thoughts, intentions and positive attitudes, the stronger your projection of energy. It's like throwing bigger rocks into the calm lake: the bigger the rocks, the bigger the waves. Now, let's say someone else comes along with similar positive energy, and you both share common ideals and goals. The combination of the two energy fields creates a larger, stronger energy projection—a bigger rock! If you toss this bigger rock into the water—the waves get higher. Try it! This simple analogy really illustrates my point. *Energy fields of the same frequency become additive, increasing the magnitude, the strength and the power of that energy, just like throwing bigger rocks into the lake.* The result is our energy is projected farther and with greater strength, just like the taller waves that reach all the way to the shore on the other side of the lake.

This coupling of positive energy is important—the energy builds upon itself. Sometimes you may be faced with goals, objectives or some type of adversity that just seems insurmountable on your own. By surrounding yourself with positive people (as in group prayer or motivational seminars), those that share your ideals, those that support you, and believe in things you believe in—your energy will be reinforced and strengthened.

As a teenager this greatly helped me to overcome the challenges I faced in the hospital and enhanced my own healing process. I used deep relaxation and meditation techniques to strengthen and focus my own energy internally, but also drew from the energy and support of those around me to increase the strength of my own energy. As an adult I continue to meditate and I consciously choose to surround myself with people who share my positive outlook on life—on both a personal and a business level. It has been a key factor in my continued success and happiness in all areas of my life. Remember—your energy and more specifically, the *frequency* of your energy field, has tremendous potential and capacity.

What about the mind—body connection? How do your health, self-confidence and self-esteem affect the energy field that you project? These are all essential ingredients for the creation of energy within all the cells of your body and for maintaining the flow of this energy throughout your body—particularly in your brain. The healthier you are; the more exercise you get and the better you eat and sleep—the stronger your energy field will be. I'm sure you've heard it said that "you are what you eat." A healthy body leads to a healthy mind. The healthier your mind is, the more efficiently the neurons in your brain are functioning, and the stronger your energy field will be. It's important to fuel your body with good, nutritional foods (remember—everything is energy, even the food you eat) exercise regularly and get plenty of sleep. These things will also contribute to a positive attitude. The energy you project is the product of your own self-confidence and self-esteem. A healthy mind, body, and attitude will all factor into your consciousness, resulting in a positive energy that is manifested in the electromagnetic field that you project outward. To put it simply: *high self-confidence and self-esteem create and project positive energy; and low self-confidence and self-esteem create and project negative energy.* Low self-esteem undermines and weakens your focus and depletes your inner energy. Since whatever you put out there is exactly what you get back—it's essential to maintain a healthy body, and a self-confident, positive attitude. Remember, the frequency of energy you project is mirrored by your physical reality and by the people around you.

If you are going through a stressful or difficult period and not feeling good about yourself—then you need to take some sort of action to purposely shift your energy. If your self-talk starts becoming negative—just consciously redirect your thoughts to a more positive internal dialogue. Force yourself to move away from the negativity. Remind yourself of the positive direction of your life, of the progress you have already made. Visualize yourself working through whatever it is that is bringing you down. Try thinking back to a more positive time when you were surrounded by loved ones, or think of something in your life right now that you appreciate. Do something you enjoy, or get some exercise; engaging in a physical activity will help you to "de-stress" and redirect your negative thoughts, and exercise will also stimulate your body to release endorphins, making you feel better instantly, It's also helpful to fill your life with music, good friends and surround yourself with positive people. When I feel stress taking over, I simply close my eyes, take a few deep breaths, and take an imaginary walk on the beach, listening to the sounds of the waves crashing on the beach… smelling the salty air… and I can feel the change immediately.

What are the things that motivate you, energize you, and make you feel whole? Jot down the things or activities that make you feel this way. Over time you will see a pattern begin to emerge. Are these things currently present in your life? If not, then make it a goal to include them in your life from now on. These things will help you to reduce stress, raise and strengthen your energy level, and achieve your own internal balance and harmony.

Try to eliminate as much stress as possible in your life. Stress breeds fear. Fear breeds confusion and hostility; which stimulates your adrenal gland to release adrenaline. The adrenaline in turn sends your heart rate and perspiration up, and the neurons in your brain begin firing at random disrupting the synchronized, orderly flow of thought patterns. This is exactly what leads to that "locked up, panicky feeling" that we've all experienced at some point in our lives during very tense and stressful situations. These physiological changes then create *more* negative energy that grows upon itself, resulting in a downward spiral of your emotions, thoughts and actions. This process is driven by both biological functions in your body and the response of your brainwave patterns to changes in your brain chemistry. The best way to handle a stressful situation is to stop, take a deep breath, and relax. Separate yourself from the cause of the stress. Once your body has begun to settle back into a normal balance, then your brain will normalize as well. As you begin to think more normally and rationally, you can then begin the process of analyzing the stress, breaking it down into its core elements, the key components that are creating the stress. Address discovering the root cause of the stress first—do a little soul searching and really look for the cause, not the symptoms. Only then can you develop an approach or plan to resolve it. This process will help to restore a balance of your energy and lead to a more positive attitude that will, in turn, shift your biological functions; lowering your blood pressure, altering your brain chemistry, and producing more endorphins and serotonin. The bottom line is: You'll get happier!

What's important here is that you develop an active approach to handling stress; one that minimizes the negativity and allows you to move through it as quickly and efficiently as possible when it does occur, with as little residual negative energy as possible. That said, it is entirely within your control to adopt and maintain a positive attitude and outlook on life, and all that it brings your way. While you may not be able to keep these "down" cycles at bay entirely, you can at least keep them to a minimum. When negative events or feelings do occur, you will be prepared (with your positive mental framework) to deal with them. Once you understand the symptoms of negative energy, and the key to combating this energy, you can learn to identify and handle it in a different way when it does arise.

There seems to be an inherent desire within most of us to control situations, and when we cannot—we often struggle with fear or anxiety about the "loss" of control. Very few of us have learned to "go with the flow." The fact is, we can *influence* people and situations, but we *cannot* control them, and the desire to control them is self-defeating and stressful. Don't try to control the world around you or the people around you... just seek a balance of your own internal positive energy and attempt to harmonize and get along with the world and people around you. You may discover that where there were once obstacles—now they are no longer there.

Here's an example: You take your dog for a walk on a leash, and he's stopping and sniffing at every tree and bush you pass. So you pull on the leash to drag and pull him in the direction that you want to go. What does your dog do? He pulls in the opposite direction! Metaphorically, what you need to do is harmonize with your dog, move in a common direction together, and communicate your desires and intentions with both your voice and the positive energy field that you project, to walk together. This may not work that well the first few times you try it, but over time you'll soon both be walking together. This analogy applies just as well to the people you interact with everyday. Trying to forcefully get others to do what you want only results in resistance, just like your dog pulling against the leash. When this occurs, take a step back mentally, reorient your thoughts and the energy pattern that you are projecting, and try to harmonize with the other person. By understanding the basis of the other person's resistance you can move towards cooperation and better communication. Your energy connects to theirs, attempting to reach a balance, as all energy naturally does. Many forms of martial arts, such as Kung Fu, utilize this same concept; where the Masters teach their students to move with the flow of the aggressive energy of their attacker rather than resisting or acting against it. By moving with this flow of energy they can throw their assailant off balance, and deflect the attack.

So let's tie these concepts together. You have to accept responsibility for your own life and your own actions, and accept that *you* are in charge of your life. Own your intentions and desires, and the choices you make. Find your personal balance and keep your energy as positive as possible. Within each of us, beneath the restless surface of our lives lies a place of deep peace and a pure energy at our core that seeks to harmonize with that of nature and the world around us.

In order to take responsibility for yourself and where you are right now, you might want to take some time to look for the patterns that tend to occur and repeat in your life—both those that are positive and negative. We learn experientially and lessons tend to repeat themselves until we really get them! Identify these patterns and those elements of your attitude and intentions that manifest in your personality, and take a good honest look at where you tend to get "stuck." Look at the external factors like your job, relationships, financial and living situations over the years—they tend to illustrate your internal patterns. By doing so, you can develop a map of your life that helps you define where you are right now and which areas of your life you might want to change or improve. Consider not only the things you want to change about your past and current patterns and behaviors, but also factor in any goals or objectives that you have. These goals may be personal, professional or simply areas of improvement in your relationships, etc. Write them down. This written landscape you're creating on paper will become a map that describes who you are, what you want out of life, and provides a direction for how you will accomplish your goals. Now, add a timeline for these goals and you will have a personal strategic plan for making some real changes and progress in your life.

As you go through the process of introspection that leads to increased self-awareness, don't confuse what you do for a living with who you really are. Many people make the mistake of defining themselves by their occupations—but your work does not define who you are or what you are; it merely defines what you do to make a living. Keep your life balanced by including hobbies and interests. Too many people find themselves retiring after working for most of their adult lives, only to discover that they have no other passions or interests, and they've forgotten who they really are. Don't let this happen to you—keep your life in balance and remember that your job is just one facet of your life.

Your personal relationships with family and friends are also an important part of your life but, they do not define who you are either. While they are important elements of your life, they only augment your identity, and hopefully they provide positive energy that contributes to your overall well being. Again, balance is important. While it is difficult to obtain, it is well worth striving for in your personal, professional, and spiritual lives. Keep in mind that your life is a journey, not just a destination. You move along a series of paths determined by the choices you make in your life, so try to make conscious choices that promote harmony and balance each day.

Balance doesn't happen overnight, and there is no time limit set here for achieving our balance. What's important is that we are actively working in a positive direction, building upon our positive energy flow, and strengthening the relationships in our lives. We want to minimize our contributions of negative energy (both internally and externally) and maximize our contributions of positive energy. Achieving a balance in our lives is challenging, and to be honest, I myself am still trying to find just the right balance—it's an ongoing effort and it requires commitment. Just like achieving success at whatever we choose to do—it takes work, it's an active process not a passive one, but the results are well worth the effort.

Follow through on your dreams by making them a part of your daily life. Believe in yourself, and believe in your dreams. Take action towards achieving your goals and dreams: Visualize them, build affirmations around them, work on finding your balance, and it will become a reality. If you are struggling to find your identity, or to find your purpose in life, don't try to force things, just listen to your inner voice. Be open to what the world around you is saying and the answers will present themselves. You will intuitively know the right answers when they come and you will find your path. Maintain a positive orientation of your thoughts, attitude, and intentions, and remember... you become what you think!

Chapter Five
The World Is Our Mirror

Every day we wake up and face an entirely new set of challenges and opportunities. We never really know for sure what life is going to throw our way on any given day. What really matters in the long run is how we handle it. If we think that life is pretty good then it probably *is* pretty good, and the world around us seems to agree. If we think that our life is terrible, or that people around us are treating us poorly, then we probably have a pretty negative attitude and the world is simply responding to our negative energy with more negativity. Ultimately we alone are responsible for the direction of our lives and accountable for our own attitude, and we always have been. The power to change our lives has always been within our reach—it's been right inside of us for all these years. Perhaps the answers you have been looking for have been right there all along, and you just didn't see them.

We each hold the key to turning our lives around, and on some level it really begins with the awareness that we *can* change our lives for the better simply by adopting a more positive attitude. Once we are aware of how our attitudes affect the energy we project, we can begin to make changes and see the results immediately. The concept is pretty straightforward: Our attitudes change the energy we project, and this energy attracts the same kind of energy from the world around us. What's happening "behind the scenes" is that the frequency of this energy we project seeks to harmonize with like frequencies of energy around us, and through this process *the world mirrors our attitudes and intentions.* The positive energy and the attitude that we project will attract positive things into our lives. Change in our lives begins with a change in our attitudes and renewed confidence in ourselves. What it really boils down to is… BE POSITIVE… and the world will respond accordingly! It really is that simple.

Early on in my career as an Aerospace Engineer I had a co-worker named Dave. Dave was a brilliant engineer that seemed able to solve virtually any type of technical problem he was given. He was truly gifted, but he had one fatal flaw. He had a negative attitude, thought everyone was out to get him, carried around a big "chip on his shoulder" and he was just plain toxic to be around. Back in the heyday of the program we worked on, the challenges and funding were abundant. Management kept Dave pretty much separated from the rest of the team with unique design problems that afforded him the isolation he desired. However, as time progressed and the program reached maturity, we began to get hit with the usual budget cutbacks. When it was time to let someone go, Dave was one of the first cuts that were made. During his last few days on the job, he made his thoughts known to everyone: He had always believed that management was out to get him, and sure enough, look what happened. He saw the world as a negative place and himself as a victim. In his mind he was victimized by management, and he perceived that it was his bad luck or fate that he was "singled out" and let go first. The reality of the situation was that his attitude created his situation: His negative energy was reflected in the world around him, and he got himself fired.

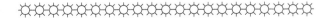

Does fate or destiny really influence our lives? There was a great line in the movie *Forrest Gump* where he said "I don't know if each of us has a destiny or if we're all just floating accidental, like on a breeze." Nobody really knows for sure if there is such a thing as fate or destiny, but here are my thoughts on the subject. If we know for a fact that the world mirrors the energy we project then where does fate or destiny come into play? Many people believe that their lives are driven by these external forces. This belief seems to absolve them of any real personal responsibility and implies that *whatever* happens in their lives (good or bad) is part of some preordained master plan set forth by God. Is God a supreme divine power who controls our fate entirely and should be credited with the good or bad things that happen in our lives? If that's the case, then where does "free will" enter the picture? These are some pretty deep questions, I know, but this concept of a supreme master plan would suggest we have no real control in the direction our lives, and that ultimately we will end up at the same place regardless of the decisions or choices we make. This concept does not allow for our individual participation in the creation of our own realities. Perhaps destiny is somehow working in the background moving our lives forward but there is no denying the fact that we have the ability to affect the direction that our lives take through the choices we make. I also happen to believe that the *best* decisions we make are those that are guided by our intuition and our connection to God or to a higher power.

The science is irrefutable, and the energy you project is measurable—you *do* affect the world around you. If you are impacting the world around you with your energy and your attitude; changing your life with each decision you make… then how can your life possibly be driven by fate or destiny alone? A belief in a God, or a belief in fate for that matter, does *not* preclude the notion that you still have some control of your own destiny. I believe that destiny and luck are really cut from the same fabric. We can't say for sure that they don't exist, but what we do know for sure is that we all have free will and our destiny or our "luck" (if there is such a thing) can be changed through the choices we make in our life. Your attitude and intentions impact your health and your well being, and they can change your physical reality. Now, accidents *do* happen, and negative cycles are indeed a part of the natural order of things, but you have far more influence over the circumstances, events, and processes through which your life unfolds than you might have previously thought. So, if fate and destiny *do* exist, you are (at the very least) co-creating your reality right along with these external forces!

Throughout these pages I have used "coincidence" and "synchronicity" pretty much interchangeably. They both describe outwardly disconnected events that occur at the same time, seemingly out of sheer chance—but that are actually laden with potential or opportunity. On the surface these events don't always appear to have any relationship, but upon further analysis they prove to be meaningful and directly correlated. I think the concept of fate and destiny is also directly related to the concept of coincidence, or synchronicity. Do coincidences really exist, or is every occurrence just part of a preordained bigger plan? As with fate and destiny, my belief is that coincidence is a combination of things. We as individuals are actively co-creating with a higher power every minute of every day. We literally draw into our lives events and circumstances that support us (often in the form of coincidences) in the direction we are moving… and perhaps fate and destiny are operating somewhere in the background, too.

I have always believed that life would bring me whatever I desired. I have believed this from a very early age, and have seen it proven time and again. I vividly remember riding my bike along the street at the age of six, hoping to catch a big dragonfly. I was fascinated by bugs and insects, and especially these big wonderful insects with multiple wings. And then, purely by chance, the biggest dragonfly I had ever seen landed right on the handlebars of my bike (I'm not making this up either)—I didn't even have to try and catch him—he came to *me*! I carefully pulled over and put him in the bug jar that I happened to have in my little backpack. I studied him, fed him bugs and let him go the next day. I was a really inquisitive child and I was completely intrigued by just about anything that could fly. A year later it was birds. I wanted one of those parrots that could talk, was reading about them every chance I could get, and pestering my parents to let me have one. Sure enough, this big black crow showed up in our yard one day, purely out of coincidence, and landed on the shed outside our kitchen window. And guess what, this big black crow could *talk*! I didn't even know crows could! He stayed around for a few days and then flew away just as suddenly as he appeared. I have seen it first hand, even as a child: *The world aligns with our energy and mirrors what we project.*

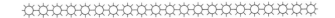

God is called by many names in many different cultures and religions across the world. The fact is that the majority of the people throughout the world believe in some form of higher power or divine energy. This belief is also shared by the majority of the world's leading scientists and physicists. For scientists, the general consensus is that this higher power (higher energy) is the same energy, which originated (as explained by the "Big Bang" Theory) when our universe was first created. *Scientists have proven that everything in the universe: all life, all matter, originated in this very moment, this "flash of light"—from a single energy source.* Interestingly, much like so many different religions around the world, the scientific communities also have different names for this ultimate energy source. Many Quantum Physicists correlate this higher source of energy that has existed since the beginning of time to the "Higgs Boson," named after Dr. Peter Higgs— who was the first to theorize a field of energy that gave certain mass to subatomic particles at extremely high temperatures in a spontaneous reaction. This "Higgs Boson" which is believed to be at the core of all energy is now also referred to by some scientists as the "God Particle!"[7] Is it possible that God and this higher energy might be one and the same?

Many scientists have dedicated their lives to the search for this divine energy, this unifying force, and a theory (coined the "theory of everything") to validate it. The new Large Hadron Collider (LHC) is the largest particle accelerator in the world and is located at the European Center for Nuclear Research (CERN) in Southern France, just outside of Geneva. CERN hosts the largest particle physics research center in the world and is made up of an extensive community that now includes over 60 countries and more than 8,000 scientists. The LHC itself is an astounding fifteen mile circular tunnel made up of huge electromagnets, where small subatomic particles travel so fast, they make 11,000 laps in a second! This facility will allow for the finishing touches on the experimental research that is expected to lead to the discovery of the Higgs Boson, among others. The LHC is now fully operational, and will begin testing in search of the Higgs Boson (ATLAS experiment) by late 2010, and according to scientists, with this device they may very well have the means to finally unlock the secrets of nature, and discover this ultimate energy source that exists at the core of all matter. The Higgs Boson or "God particle" is exactly what they hope to find.

Some exciting doors have been opened in the scientific world in the last fifty years. As new discoveries have been made, we have seen an increasing convergence of science (specifically quantum physics) with the philosophies of the Eastern mystics, those that have been refined over a 2500-year history. As we progress into the next century we expect to see an acceleration of this convergence as more answers are discovered in the world of science, and as our knowledge grows about ourselves and the world around us. As our technology continues to advance, so will our insight and understanding of this ultimate energy source—in whatever form we may uncover. Whatever we choose to call it, scientists, spiritualists and most religions seem to agree that there *is* a higher source of energy at the core of everything and everyone. From a personal perspective, I do believe in a supreme energy, and I believe that God, by any name—be it scientific or religious, *is* this energy source. I also believe that this energy can be channeled to do miraculous things, and, most importantly, that each of us possesses this very same energy!

Many faiths throughout the world worship through prayer. Prayer, in its many forms is another way (like meditation) of changing our internal energy patterns—thereby changing the frequency of the energy that we project into the world. It can also be a powerful means of self-transformation. Our prayers create a synchronized consciousness, increasing our energy field as the result of our focused, organized thought patterns connecting to the network of energy around us. When we pray our minds are calm, our thoughts are focused and our intentions are clear. Whether we are praying for guidance, forgiveness, help with a personal issue, or simply expressing gratitude for our good fortunes—the very act of prayer opens our minds and projects an energy field that embodies our thoughts and intentions. This energy is vibrating at a defined frequency that often times will attract into our lives the very thing we are praying for. When we hear of people's prayers being answered, we often interpret this as a result of divine intervention or an alignment of the world around the prayer, and perhaps it is a little of both. We know for a fact that group prayer significantly increases the energy projected—because so many minds are operating together with a single minded focus and intent. In fact, group prayer has proven to be so effective that it has even been credited with reducing crime rates in many major cities, including Washington D.C.. Organized studies have actually been conducted in several major cities across the country, and they have shown that with large, organized group prayer efforts—crime rates have directly been impacted, in some cases dropping up to twenty-five percent in the participating cities. There is definitely power in numbers and the strength of the combined energy is always more than the sum of its individual parts.

Personally, I have always thought of the projection of my own energy more along the lines of a projection of my "will power." My professional career began as an Aerospace engineer (yes, I'm a "rocket scientist" but I promise to keep the scientific jargon to a minimum) and I've always loved science and had a great curiosity about the world around me, so this was a natural direction for me to take in both my education and my career. I was frequently conflicted between my belief in science and my deep spiritual beliefs, knowing that I had personally experienced at least two miracles. I've always had a very strong desire to reconcile the scientific facts with my spiritual beliefs, and what I knew intuitively to be true. The energy that I had tapped into to heal my own body when I was young was real. I knew it, I saw the results! Much of my adult life has been spent trying to understand the "how and why" behind this very energy, and to explore the true purpose that my life may have.

For many years I worked as an engineer on some of the nation's most secretive, high tech programs that existed, and I excelled at this type of scientific work. Over time, I discovered that I also had a unique ability to convince people that my particular technical approach, solution or design, was the right way to go. Certainly, it wasn't always the case, but it proved out more often than not. I was promoted quickly to senior positions within the programs I worked on and eventually became program manager of many. Business development and marketing were also interests of mine and talents I had developed, and my career soon moved in that direction, with great success. I ultimately translated these skills from individual projects, to programs, and then to running businesses. I thrived on the challenge of taking a business, creating a strategic plan, and working with the company's executive team and staff to implement the plan, thus allowing the company to grow to its fullest potential. The process of taking a business and helping it grow and live up to its fullest potential is very much in keeping with the concepts and information contained here in these pages! What works for us on an individual level also works on a larger scale! The same principles apply. I knew from an early age that when I applied myself things seemed to always go my way; instinctively I felt that I could actually make things happen simply by focusing hard on the results I wanted. Whether it was charisma, luck, or talent, I was able to translate this ability (refined over many years), into a very successful business career. I honestly feel that the success I have experienced in my own career is essentially the result of a positive attitude. My commitment, passion, motivation, focus, and strength of will were without question, influential. I believed in myself, worked hard, and made things happen. I found that during presentations this confidence (or charisma) was especially influential. Through intense focus I could reach a highly charged state of consciousness where I could uniquely connect with the people around me, reaching a "zone" where I could almost feel the energy reaching out to my audience. In times like that when I was "connecting" with people, the words just flowed. Ultimately, I believe that my positive energy was behind my successes!

Try harnessing your own energy and exploring the things that interest or inspire you further. Let your intuition guide you and pay attention to the coincidences in your life, too. They may contain opportunities for future growth or even future careers. You are not automatically slated to have one single career or profession—in fact one career often leads to another, and there is value in whatever you are passionate about... whatever you love to do. Because I love to fly, I took lessons, ended up obtaining my pilot's license, then my commercial pilot's license and eventually teaching others to fly (as a flight instructor) as well. Sometimes your "hobbies" can even become a career. There is an energy frequency behind everything you do, and if you are doing what you love, the universe will mirror that positive energy and you will be supported and successful in your endeavors. Find what you love to do... and do it!

The direction and quality of your life is something that you can control to a large degree. You control your thoughts, your intentions, your attitude, and whether you change your attitude through the power of prayer and belief in a supreme being, change your attitude through meditation or change your thoughts and intentions through sheer force of will, you are making a change in the energy you project. This change in your own attitude is what will ultimately change your life. Remember, your thoughts, attitudes, and intentions will alter the pattern of energy in your brain, change your brain chemistry, and ultimately the pattern of energy that you project. By keeping your attitude and intentions positive, the people and world around you (as well as your physical reality) will respond accordingly, often through what you perceive as coincidence.

Coincidences happen all the time and we can all relate to them. We have all had occasions where we've been thinking of someone, perhaps a family member or friend, the phone rings and sure enough, it's that very person on the phone that you were just thinking about… coincidence, right? You can probably also think of a coincidental event or experience you've had that ended up having a pivotal impact on your life. For example: If you are in a relationship: How did you meet the person you are currently with? You had to be in the right place at the right time to make that personal connection and you listened to your intuition that this could be a meaningful person in your life. Your life changed as a result. Opportunities present themselves to you on a regular basis in the form of what we would interpret to be coincidence. Your energy is reaching out into the world around you and connecting with other energy via the Higgs field. This is the underlying science behind coincidence.

Are you ever left with a feeling that certain meetings with people, interactions, or events that occur in your life can't possibly be just luck or chance? Well you're exactly right. This synchronicity that occurs in your life is largely a result of the projection of your intentions, thoughts and attitude; all translated into an energy field that other people and the world around you respond to. Your energy can draw these people into your life, or precipitate an event or occurrence, as a result of your energy harmonizing with the energy of the world around you.

This happens all of the time, but most of us miss these coincidental connections because we are too busy, or too focused on something else going on that we are unaware of them. Just recently, my daughter was feeling mentally drained after hours in her architecture studio class. She was struggling to come up with an idea for an environmental design on a building project that was supposed to combine nature with the existing structures on Alcatraz Island. The city of San Francisco was in the process of converting some elements of the island into a national park and they wanted to integrate what was already there with new environmental structures to bridge the history of the island. This was the goal of her project. She was at a real loss for design ideas. On her way home from the studio, she decided to stop off at Noah's bagel shop on Telegraph for a latte. Once situated there with her coffee, she stopped struggling mentally with the task before her and she just sat there quietly, looking out the window, drifting in thought. It was a beautiful, brisk afternoon. Students and couples strolled by and the local street vendors bantered with the tourists hoping to encourage a purchase. She found herself relaxing and enjoying the moment. A flock of pigeons flew past and she watched as most of them landed on the roof of the building across the street, while others perched on the flags circling the rooftops that were blowing in the gentle breeze. In that moment, inspiration struck. A design idea came to her in its entirety. It was an aviary structure that integrated the concept of sails on a ship, with the sharp angular designs of the cliffs configured for seating areas where tourists could pause and sit to view the local birds characteristic of the rock island (Alcatraz is also known as "Bird Island"). Suddenly she had her answer! Her subconscious mind had focused on a problem she was trying to solve and even as she quieted her mind, she was projecting an energy field outward that aligned with her external world, coincidence… right? When our minds are quieted, clarity of our thought processes will occur. I have often experienced sudden flashes of insight or thoughts that pop into my head at night just before I drift off to sleep. For me, this is a time when my mind is still, and insight and inspiration can make their way to the surface. I try to keep a notepad by the bed for this very reason—some of my best insights and ideas have come to me in those moments just before sleep!

Some coincidences in life are very subtle, and they often occur without our even being aware of them. They can involve people, events, experiences, concepts, ideas or things. The coincidence itself isn't what's necessarily important; it's the opportunity, message or meaning behind the coincidence. It's really about the value of the connection made; the potential impact to our lives that this intersection could possibly have. The interaction may occur in a very short period of time, but the insight we walk away with, or the influence the event may have on us, can be life changing. As the famous physicist Albert Einstein once said, "God does not throw dice, nothing happens by accident." Modern quantum physicists have indeed proven that all phenomena we perceive is the result of this energy that exists within us, all around us, and flows through all matter that exists. These coincidences are a manifestation of the energy we project interacting with the energy in the world around us. The phenomena we readily perceive with our five senses; sight, sound, smell, hearing and touch, are a product of interaction with different forms of this same energy. *In order to recognize synchronicity or coincidence at work in our lives, we need to look beyond our five senses, we need to perceive intuitively, and we do this only through our connection to the very energy we are made of.* Remember, this same energy is interwoven and interconnected (via the Higgs field) in a vast network that stretches across the entire universe.

The concepts of synchronicity and coincidence, and their correlation to the interactions of our energy fields, have fascinated the great minds in science and religion for many hundreds of years. Eastern mystics and ancient philosophers have long held that all people and everything that exists in the universe are intimately connected. They also believe that the coincidences in our lives *do* carry meaning, although the meaning may not always be readily clear or apparent at the time. Carl Jung, a famous analytical psychologist spent much of his career studying synchronicity, specifically working to tie the energy of the subconscious mind to the events and occurrences in our lives that were of significance or somehow provided guidance. Jung suggests that "a unique interdependence exists among events that correlate to the state of mind of the people involved in the coincidental experience." Jung's analysis of coincidence was the result of a lifetime of studying the behavior of people and evaluating synchronous occurrences in the subjects he had interviewed. The results of his research suggest that "random occurrences are related to our state of mind, which represents the charged energy state of the mind of the two people experiencing the coincidence."[6] What this implies is that *our* state of mind, and the energy we project, has a direct influence on the events that occur around us. This certainly supports our previous conclusions about energy projection.

In his book, *Comprehending Coincidence*, Craig Bell suggests that there are two basic types of coincidences that we can experience: "mirror" coincidences and "directional" coincidences. According to Bell, "coincidences often suggest a deeper meaning to our lives, opportunity for guidance or direction." Mirror coincidences *reflect* the focus of the mind that is highly charged with energy, illustrating the way our external world mirrors the energy that we are projecting. Directional coincidences are also related to the state of mind of the individual and they seem to offer more concrete *direction or guidance*. In both cases, the challenge, of course, is to actually recognize that a coincidence has occurred, and to be open and receptive to any meaning or guidance that this coincidence provides. Bell eloquently relates these concepts to a variety of explanations and examples. He also goes on to describe the mind as a "magnet… with the forces that we project resulting in events which offer either mirror or directional coincidences."[8]

Frijtof Capra seems to concur. In *The Tao of Physics*, he explains that "the interconnectedness of all matter across the universe, both organic and inorganic, is accomplished through a vast network of energy that exists all around us, flows through us and makes up all that exists across the universe."[9] This concept of a vast network of energy (also expressed throughout Eastern philosophies) further strengthens the notion that the energy field we project reaches out into the world and attracts "like" frequencies of energy. Now let's put these two concepts together:

1. *Each of us creates and projects an energy field.*
2. *A vast network of energy exists that connects us all together.*

As a natural result of this, coincidences occur in our lives through this connection of energy that exists all around us. Due to the very properties of energy itself and the connectedness of this energy—we have the capacity to mold our physical reality in a direction defined by our thoughts and intentions. Think about it. We can, and *do* influence the people and events around us through the projection of an energy field that is created by our conscious and subconscious minds. We influence what happens in the world around us, including our own physical wellbeing, by our thoughts, attitudes and intentions. The world mirrors these attitudes and intentions—whether positive or negative; it mirrors our energy field and the frequency of that energy. Again, this mirroring process is often manifested in the synchronicity and coincidences that appear in our lives. These coincidences occur as the world around us matches the frequency of our own charged energy, resulting in people or events that may provide some guidance, lesson or support… all based upon the focused energy that embodies our thoughts and intentions.

Here's what's happening. The more you focus, the stronger your energy field becomes. When your mind is filled with noise from the outside world, when you are distracted, or your mind is cluttered with issues, conflict or stress; the energy you project becomes weak and unfocused. As a child did you ever do the sidewalk experiment using dry leaves and a magnifying glass on a sunny day? By directing the sun's rays through the magnifying glass and onto the leaves they are focused into a single powerful point of light (and energy) and if you get the point of light focused tightly enough, the leaves will begin to smolder and burn. Taking the scattered light (energy) of the sun and focusing it into that single pinpoint makes it far more powerful—almost like a laser beam! The focus of your mind and your energy works in much the same way. Your conscious and subconscious mind is always in gear, and both of them influence the projection of your energy field. If your mind is "noisy" then your energy is scattered and weaker and your awareness is limited. Conversely, when your mind is calm, and external noise reduced to a minimum, the energy you project becomes more focused and stronger, and you become much more aware of your connection to the world around you. In these moments; when you are in the "zone," your synchronicity with the world around you is far more apparent, and you are far more open to any coincidences that may occur. When your mind is calm, the neurons in your brain across both left and right hemispheres are actually linked electrically through a network that connects them (across the corpus collosum, for example) allowing you to project a more cohesive energy field that is much stronger, and more closely correlated to the focus of your intentions. The external world not only picks up this energy from a greater distance, but also tends to reflect your intentions much more closely. It is important to maintain a clear, calm, focused mind and remain open to the synchronicity in your life.

Remember the example I used in the previous chapter. Think again of your thoughts and intentions as being the rock that you toss out into a calm lake. It creates rings of circular waves that project out from the point at which the rock hits the water. These waves represent the energy created by your thoughts and intentions as they ripple outward into the external world. Single, focused thoughts are like a nice, big rock—they will create a stronger, clearer pattern of (energy) waves on a calm lake. Now, imagine that it's a really windy day and the lake is no longer smooth, but choppy with little white caps. When you toss your rock into this choppy (noisy) lake, the waves your rock creates are swallowed up and virtually canceled out by the "noise" of the other waves on the lake. This same thing happens to the energy you project. We live in a busy, hectic world that is already filled with noise and beyond that we still have to deal with life challenges, family, and work issues. The noise of the world along with the noise in our minds will dilute our focus along with the strength of the energy we project. When this happens and coincidences do occur, most of us miss all but the most overt ones because our minds are so clouded with distractions. If we aren't projecting clear or coherent energy, then the world cannot respond in a clear or coherent way either. Your energy field is always far more powerful when you are coming from a place of clarity, quiet and focus.

So, the question arises: If we are affecting our external reality and the world is responding to our energy, then why do "bad" things happen to "good" people? Are we creating every situation that arises? When I broke my neck or was involved in that car accident was I somehow projecting some kind of energy subconsciously that precipitated these accidents? Was my sister? Of course not, but accidents and negative events do happen. In my own circumstances, I found that I could improve the situation by my response to it. Remember, it is how we *deal* with our challenges and adversity in life that defines us. Many of the events that followed the accidents I experienced were the result of my highly charged psyche. It was as though the world instantly aligned and responded with a series of coincidences that effectively took me in the right direction—events that had a profound effect on my recovery. I can look back now and see that they were indeed significant and they did provide both guidance and insight that would continue to impact me throughout my life. Each event taken individually would appear random, but together they comprise a series of very deliberate and meaningful events.

Jung says, "One's state of mind at the time of occurrence will determine if we recognize the coincidence. Our state of mind establishes the basis for understanding the significance, either in the context of our conscious or subconscious thoughts, or in the context of our life's journey at that particular point in time."[6] He goes on to suggest that our mind (which is where our intentions and thoughts are focused) will draw in or attract similar types of energy. When our minds are focused intently on something we are projecting an energy which acts like a *magnet* to attract occurrences or people that are in turn generating a similar type of energy. What Jung is referring to is exactly what we have been talking about here—he is referring to the projection of electromagnetic energy created in our minds, the result of the electrical energy generated by the millions of neurons all firing in our brains which automatically entrains similar energy in our immediate physical reality.

I believe that our paths must often cross with people that can create value in our lives and provide insight and direction, and I am sure that many of these go unnoticed if we are not open to them or receptive at that particular moment. After "semi-retiring" at a relatively young age I took up flying in a serious way and ultimately became both a commercial pilot and flight instructor. One of my students, Jeff, discovered during our many cockpit conversations, that I had a background in "growing" businesses, and asked for some advice on the operations of his golf company. I must have hit some hot buttons because he eventually hired me out of early retirement to run that company and to help with several of his other projects. Because of our mutual interest in flying, it was pure coincidence that Jeff and I crossed paths. Interestingly enough, he was also a catalyst for the writing of this book. It turned out that he had co-authored several of the *Chicken Soup for the Soul* books. Jeff thought I had an energetic and positive attitude and suggested that

I try my hand at writing a motivational book. Our coincidental connection has benefited both of us in many ways: He has found someone that can significantly increase the size and value of his business endeavors; I am fulfilling a personal goal by writing this book, *and* I'm really enjoying the process of expanding his businesses, too. This kind of synchronicity has occurred frequently throughout my life, and while I am sure that I have missed many coincidences and opportunities in my life—those I am aware of have left a profound impact on me.

In both my personal life and my professional career, people have always seemed to cross paths with me at just the right time. I've also had a few "life saving" coincidences. As a business development executive I spent much of my life (fifteen years or so) traveling—sleeping in hotels, running through airports and watching the clouds pass below as I zigzagged back and forth across the country. I have had my share of missed flights and delayed connections throughout my career, but there are two flights in particular that I will always remember; flights I was booked on and ultimately missed or changed, that ended in disaster. The first one was when I missed a night flight into Los Angeles from Chicago. I was tied up in traffic heading to the airport and I got to the gate after the flight had already left, forcing me to take the next flight out. The plane I was originally scheduled to take ended up colliding with a small commuter plane (that had entered the runway at the wrong time) on landing in Los Angeles. Several people were killed and many were hurt. I walked in the door several hours late to a distraught wife who was still awake—glued to the television watching the local news… she had my previous flight information and I hadn't called when I missed the flight.

The second time this happened also had an impact on me. I frequently traveled to Washington D.C. for business meetings, and

I was there for a quick one day trip on a Monday. I was scheduled to return home the next morning on the Dulles to Los Angeles flight, but my daughter had a school function that I wanted to attend and I was eager to get back home and sleep in my own bed. So, rather than taking the flight I was scheduled on that next morning, I changed my reservation and jumped on the six o'clock evening flight from Dulles to L.A. I got in very late that Monday night and consequently I slept in later than usual the next day. I awoke to my wife running into the bedroom that morning to tell me what had just happened. The date was Sept 11th, 2001. Had I not changed my reservation and gotten on that earlier flight I could have been on one of those flights that were hijacked.

I have often been referred to as being incredibly lucky and incredibly blessed. In most cases I couldn't agree more. My point with these last few examples is that I do believe that we can also create our own luck, and that often the things we perceive to be luck, or being in the right place at the right time, are really coincidences that occur in part as a byproduct of our highly charged minds. It's hard to argue the existence of divine intervention when a miracle seems to have occurred, or when there simply is no other explanation for something happening. Again, I can relate to this personally. Life is funny that way, sometimes we just *can't* explain why things happen. When we find ourselves faced with this dilemma we fall back on our faith and continue with our lives. I for one am a firm believer in miracles; I have experienced them first hand.

Make a commitment to be positive, stay open to the possibilities in your life and open to coincidences. The psychic mental energy that you project connects to the world around you and mirrors energy of similar frequency that manifests in events or people that cross your path as you progress on your life's journey. When you notice coincidences occurring in your life—write them down in a daily journal so that you can come back and reflect on the potential meaning or direction that may be hidden there. You can analyze what you think is being communicated or record what was going on in your mind at that moment, and think about the inference or meaning before taking action or making a decision. Their intended meaning is not always immediately clear, however. Hindsight is said to be "twenty-twenty," and sometimes years may go by before you can really appreciate the synchronicity that has taken place in your life. You can probably look back now and think of a time or situation where coincidence played a critical role in the events that transpired or changed your life.

The energy field we project can also manifest itself in the law of attraction: one of the universal laws of nature that (simply put) states "like attracts like." We attract people into our lives that are drawn to our energy, and attracted to the attitudes that we project. Our personal relationships are a great example of the law of attraction at work. When we feel good about life and about ourselves and we feel a strong positive connection with someone else's energy, it means the frequencies of our energy fields are in harmony and there is a mutual "attraction." Our positive thoughts and energy attract similar energy. Similarly, if we have low self-esteem, a bad attitude or we are projecting anger or dissatisfaction, then our negative energy field will attract negative relationships and situations.

Take a look at the relationships you now have in your life and objectively ask yourself if they are positive or negative. Have you consistently attracted negative or unhealthy relationships into your life? The best way to change your relationships with other people is to start with your relationship with yourself. By developing a positive attitude and self-image you will exude a more confident, positive outlook and you will begin to attract healthier, positive people and situations into your life.

Prayer, meditation, clearly defined goals and objectives, affirmations, and even our hopes and dreams all serve a similar purpose. They are tools that we can use every day to quiet our minds and focus our energy. Through the use of these tools we can shift our mind set from negative to positive and we can retune the frequency of the energy we project into a more positive energy field that will improve the quality of our lives. Our lives are filled with many variables, and we are bombarded on a daily basis with negative energy. There are times when it's all we can do to just get out of bed and go to work. On days like this we just have to try to avoid internalizing any more of the negative energy and focus on the positive aspects of our lives instead. We can learn to manage the flow of negative influences and information in our lives… and keep our focus on the positive. No matter how dismal things may appear, there is always *something* to be grateful for. Gratitude is another great way to shift your energy quickly back into the positive zone. Life *is* a journey, and things just don't always turn out exactly the way we might have hoped or planned, but that's also the beauty of life—each day holds something new and unexpected.

You may be asking yourself, "Why should I even try to maintain this positive attitude if the results aren't certain?" The answer is this: Because the probability of your prayers being answered, of you meeting your goals and objectives, and the probability of great things in your life turning out as you had hoped and dreamed is far, far higher if you have a highly charged, positive mental attitude and you are willing to make it happen. If you are cynical or closed off to the idea of trying something new, how can you grow and evolve in this lifetime? You have to learn to be open and willing to take some risks in order to move forward in life. You have nothing to lose and everything to gain! Imagine; if you never opened yourself up to falling in love because you were afraid of getting hurt, then you would miss out on the elation of mind and spirit that accompanies being in love!

It's a fact, and science backs it up. When your attitude is positive and your mind highly charged with positive energy, the endorphin and serotonin levels in your body and your brain chemistry are *all* changed. These changes directly influence your health and mental well being. All of these factors contribute to directly changing the frequency of energy that you project. The resulting positive energy field helps bring the world into alignment and the world around you attempts to harmonize with the frequency of energy that you project. The results you desire will manifest in your reality. As you reach your goals, and see your hopes and dreams becoming reality, your resolve will continue to strengthen and your awareness will continue to grow. These positive events affirm and validate your connection and your direction in life.

The Eastern religious philosophies as well as modern quantum physics; all acknowledge and reference a connected network of energy throughout the universe. Sometimes we have those rare mystical moments that offer us glimpses of the true oneness of the universe, confirming our inner knowledge that a higher power is at work across the universe. These moments provide a genuine feeling of connection to God, and in these moments we can instantly relate to the value and importance of the synchronicity in our lives. We've all, at some point had these glimpses; perhaps while alone on a morning walk with the sun just coming up; or looking out onto a lake with the wisps of fog floating above the surface of the calm water on a cold, crisp morning, or looking up at the stars on a moonless night—in awe of the heavens above. When we feel this oneness, an almost eerie sense of calm flows over us, we close our eyes, and for a moment we can literally *feel* a connection, a flow of energy, within ourselves and with nature all around us. Stargazing does it for me every time—it humbles, inspires and amazes me, and I always feel my connection to the universe in these moments. *If you haven't done this for a while, do yourself a favor; turn the television set off, throw a blanket down on the lawn tonight and treat yourself to an evening of inspiration… it's good for your body, mind and spirit!*

You may have felt this same rush of calm, or of oneness with a loved one when being held; your eyes closed, and as you exhaled and relaxed in the embrace, you felt suddenly at one with that person, completely safe, as though nothing else existed in the world around you. Many would characterize this as an almost mystical experience. It always is for me. Now, you may not be overlooking a lake right now, or gazing at the stars, but the feeling, the experience is undeniable. This rush of calmness that flows through you is a result of your energy field harmonizing with the energy of nature around you. Do you remember falling in love and staying up nearly all night talking with this other person, and waking the next day after only a few hours of sleep—still feeling alive and energetic? This is a perfect example that we can all directly relate to; it illustrates that rush of energy flowing through your body, magnified by the harmony with nature, or with the other person. I remember just after my son A.J. was born, holding him in my arms; his chubby little face close to mine. I closed my eyes. I could feel his warm breath on my cheeks and I felt his little heart beating… my own heart beat was exactly the same rhythm. I felt connected to him, strangely connected to myself, and I felt as though our energy; our souls were one and the same. In that instant I was reminded of the precious gift of life, and I felt an intimate connection to my very own little universe, a connection that I share with both of my children to this very day. Wouldn't it be incredible to feel this way all of the time!

We sometimes find ourselves struggling with the notion of our value in life, not only to our families but to the rest of humankind. We want to matter, and to make a difference. It's human nature that we all want to have a purpose; we want our lives to have meaning and value. We want our lives to stand for something meaningful and we don't want to just wake up every day, go to work, come home, watch television until we fall asleep and repeat the process day in and day out.

If you find yourself wanting to live a more purposeful life, start by believing in yourself. Trust that you will indeed find your path. Remember, you are connected to the entire universe! Every single coincidence that occurs in your life is absolutely ripe with possibilities and the guidance and direction you seek *will* come. Follow your intuition, and listen to your inner voice. When you follow your heart, you will feel your energy flow and guide you in a positive direction, helping you to reach your potential.

꙰꙰꙰꙰꙰꙰꙰꙰꙰꙰꙰꙰꙰꙰꙰꙰꙰꙰꙰꙰

Over the last several years, the world has been thrust into chaos; not just by the state of the global economy and environmental concerns such as global warming, but also by the very differences amongst cultural relationships across national borders, and growing conflicts that have arisen from those differences. In some cases the very survival of many people is being called into question. These conditions push our sense of reality to its limits, and force us to reassess our values and priorities. I believe that the state of affairs of our nation and indeed the global situation may very well serve as a catalyst for extraordinary change—an evolutionary transformation that will reshape the human experience. Never before in the history of mankind have we seen such powerful validation that we are all connected. We are connected not just from an economic perspective, but from an environmental and spiritual perspective as well. These facts have been proven to us many times in this decade alone. The only way that we can affect changes at the global level, and change the direction of the course that we are currently on, is to recognize and embrace the interconnectedness of the universe and of all that exists within it. We cannot simply act blindly or independently any longer. We are part of a global community and our very survival is at stake.

Human evolution will only progress when we are ready to accept that we are all part of a larger whole. We are now being forced to recognize just how instantly and intimately connected we all are, and how what we do in one country directly affects the lives of people in other countries across the globe. The human species (along with all other living organic matter) has evolved in subtle ways over the last centuries, as a course of survival against the elements. We have made great technological advances as well, but we have been irresponsible in many ways; operating without regard for the planet as a whole. We are now undergoing an evolution of our psychic, emotional and intellectual reality as a consequence of our interactions with nature and with each other.

The events we are now experiencing will result in changes within each of us. Changes in the way we think, changes in the way we interact with each other, changes in the way we take action to change the world around us. I believe a shift in the world order, a massive awakening of our awareness is underway, and with this awareness comes hope for our future. No longer can we remain isolated; our survival in the generations to come will be driven by our awareness and acceptance of the interconnectedness of all energy that flows through us and around us, and most importantly by our cooperation and synchronicity with this flow of energy.

As we each embrace this energy individually, and reach a level of harmony within ourselves and with the immediate world around us; a global momentum will begin to build. I believe the human race will soon reach a tipping point in our global awareness, driven by the combined strength of our individual energy projections. The human race, synchronized in positive energy and unified in our commitment to transcend our current dilemmas, will harmonize once again with nature around us. I truly believe that the chaos we are witnessing throughout the world right now will serve as the catalyst for sweeping change in the way we all interact and connect. Thus, the healing process for our global economy, for our environment, and for the human condition will begin. Remember, the energy that is projected by our conscious and subconscious minds is interacting and reaching out for energy of the same frequency. The world mirrors the energy we project and together, collectively, we can change the course of the path we are on.

Change your own attitude, thoughts and intentions; change the energy field that you project, and you will change your world. Be positive. Your physical reality will reflect the energy you project; perhaps slowly at first, but the momentum will build as your positive energy builds and strengthens. So, be true to yourself, know yourself, and know that change begins with what you believe and how you think. Whatever life brings you—no matter the challenges, embrace the change, the opportunities that present themselves, and remain committed to living each day purposefully and completely. Become aware of the energy you project, aware of the synchronicity and coincidences that occur in your life, and be open to the symbolism, meaning and guidance that may be presented.

Our attitudes are the catalyst for our own personal changes, and they will be the catalyst for change on a global level as well. Attitude changes our perspective in life; it changes how we feel, it changes how we think life treats us. Attitude changes our perception of the world around us *and* how the world perceives and reacts to us. A positive attitude spontaneously blooms into positive results. We *can* change the world, one person at a time. As Norman Vincent Peale wrote in his well known book, *The Power of Positive Thinking*, "Live life with no regrets, think positively about the attainment of your particular desires and they will be achieved, the mind is a powerful tool, and the fact that positive visualization can lead to positive results is almost ridiculously self evident."[10] There are volumes of information that point to the value of positive thinking, and it is validated in a multitude of life stories and examples told by people around the world.

Unfortunately, many of us just can't seem to really integrate this knowledge about the power of our thoughts and attitudes into everyday life. Something gets lost in translation and while we intellectually know that positive thinking works, we just can't seem to practice it ourselves or stick with it long enough to see the results. We have a setback and we give up, or the time it seems to take to get the results we want just seems interminably long. As I have said— positive thinking *can* change your life and your physical reality. My friend, Randi used positive thinking, visualization and her faith to heal her own body of cancer. Against all odds, by combining Eastern wisdom and Western science and technology with her persistence and sheer determination—she was able to overcome this disease and she is a testament to the strength and ability of our minds and spirits to overcome adversity. She underwent treatments at Beth Israel Deaconess Medical Center (a teaching hospital of Harvard Medical School) in Boston and they published the following article (by Julia Cruz) about her story in 2009:

Surviving Cancer with Faith, Focus and CyberKnife

As a financial advisor, Randi Meryl helps her clients grow their assets and secure their financial future. But her own future was very much in doubt three years ago when she was diagnosed with potentially deadly lung cancer.

"I was hiking with a friend, and suddenly couldn't catch my breath," says the avid athlete and marathon runner. "I'm really strong, but I just didn't feel right." Her doctor initially diagnosed her with a nasal infection, but after a few weeks, it still hadn't cleared. Eventually she went to the emergency room. Chest X-rays and a CAT-scan revealed a 10-centimeter mass in her right lung that was pressing on her superior vena cava vein and restricting blood flow from her head.

"I was in shock," recalls Randi. "They immediately admitted me to the hospital. It was really frightening." A battery of tests revealed Randi had small cell lung cancer—a disease in which malignant cancer cells form in the tissue of the lungs. Her doctors told her the cancer was inoperable and would be very difficult to cure—even with chemotherapy and radiation.

A practicing Buddhist for thirty years, Randi turned to her faith to deal with the news. Rather than being devastated, she was determined to live. "My feeling was… give me what you got. I'll try anything," says Randi. "I focused on, 'What do we have to do next?' That's the way I am. I kept telling my doctor, "I just want a shot at this" She began chemo and radiation treatments, undaunted by the knowledge that the treatments are only curative for her form of cancer about 15-30% of the time. It was long and grueling—thirty-five days of radiation, six rounds of chemo. When her blood cell count dropped so low doctors told Randi they would have to stop the chemo, she didn't give in. Instead, she focused on her faith.

"I chanted and chanted about it and the next morning my white blood cell count was back up. I was not going to miss a session. I was so determined to keep going," she remembers. Her determination paid off. By the end of her first round of treatments, the tumor had shrunk dramatically and Randi's prognosis was looking better. She'd been through so much physically and emotionally and wanted to connect with others who understood her experience., so she started her own painting classes for cancer patients, both to "give back to the community" and as a kind of group therapy. "I think people felt they needed to pay attention to something else besides their cancer," Randi recalls. "One woman told me, 'I don't get off my couch all week long, but I can come to your class.' We didn't so much talk about cancer or our stories, but we would do visualizations to connect to our 'Chi' or inner spirit before we would start to paint. People would leave the class with more energy and enthusiasm and a nice painting. They always said they felt so much better afterwards."

Randi felt better too. She was getting stronger and stronger each day. Then in April of 2008 a PET-scan revealed a re-growth of the original tumor in her lung. The cancer was back. Her doctors told her chemo wouldn't be enough to destroy the cancer this time, but there was one other option. CyberKnife—a leading edge medical technology that pinpoints tumors better than other treatments and kills cancer cells without destroying a lot of healthy tissue. The doctors from different hospitals worked together to get Randi the best medical treatment possible.

"We'd performed dozens of CyberKnife treatments for non-small cell cancer, but had not used it for small cell cancer when I met Randi,"

recalls Dr. Stuart Berman, radiation oncologist at BIDMC. "But she was a youthful fifty-year-old in excellent physical shape and her persistence convinced us to give it a try. After discussing her case with Dr. Willers we decided to go ahead with CyberKnife treatment." "It was amazing," Randi recalls. Three weeks after her treatments started, Randi underwent follow up radiology tests and got the news she'd been hoping for. The cancer was in remission. It was the day before Thanksgiving. "It was really beautiful—a tremendous relief. I knew it was going to work. I wasn't surprised, but I was really relieved. We did it," says Randi. Today, Randi remains in remission and is feeling great. She's still teaching Chinese brush painting to fellow cancer survivors and credits her husband Richard, her friends, her faith and the staff at Beth Israel Deaconess Medical Center for helping her through her own diagnosis and treatment. Randi stresses that "cancer is an individual battle that takes faith, discipline and persistence to overcome. You have to make an effort. When you train for a marathon you have to put in the time and the effort and fighting cancer is the same," Randi notes. "With cancer it's steps—you get to the first wall and have to figure out how to get around it. Every step is a victory that takes you to the next step. We have to say to ourselves, "Never give up."[11]

Why is it that some of us find a way to overcome our challenges—no matter how daunting, and some of us simply give up when faced with major life hurdles? Obviously, those of us who stay positive and stay focused on our ultimate goals have a distinct advantage. We also have to be willing to do the work. We have to actively participate in moving past whatever barriers we encounter in our lives. It's far too easy to throw in the towel and give up if we lose sight of the big picture of our life's journey, so keeping our goals in mind is essential. We can't let ourselves get so caught up in our unconscious routines that we lose sight of who we really are or what our real priorities are.

In the process of chasing the paycheck, trying to just stay ahead of things, being in relationships, and taking care of our families; we can easily lose our own identities. When this happens, subconsciously we begin to feel dissatisfied or unhappy. Negative energy inside of us begins to build and it can eat away at any positive energy that we have. Eventually, this negativity can dominate the energy we project and result in an attraction of similar energy from the world around us. A snowball effect occurs and it can easily manifest as a perception that everything around us is going from bad to worse! If we lose our center and our sense of self, then we aren't able to renew and refresh the positive energy at our core, and the negative energy is allowed to run rampant!

Don't let things get away from you like this. It's important to take a few minutes out at the end of each day just for you. Take the time to quiet your mind and acknowledge the good things in your life, those things that make you feel happy and content. Allow yourself some time away from distractions, where you can reflect, and center yourself. This is vitally important. The more hectic your life, the more important this becomes. For me, this time of quiet reflection is in the last few moments at night, my head on the pillow, just before I drift off to sleep.

The present moment is a gift. Cultivating contentment in our lives allows us to appreciate that gift, to appreciate who we are, and to see value in whatever it is that we do. Each day is filled with potential, and each day presents new opportunities and possibilities. Every event or coincidence that occurs in our lives, every goal that we accomplish, or new person that we meet could represent a potential new beginning, a new direction or path for our life's journey. Renew your own internal energy, allow time for quiet contemplation, and calm your mind so that you minimize internal conflicts. Stay balanced in your life, keep your positive energy high; and your thoughts, intentions and desires will be similarly reflected in your health, job, and relationships. Setbacks are normal. Don't let them get you down—just push on through the negativity and, keep a positive, centered, sense of self. Maintain a positive attitude and your energy will follow, the world will align with you and amazing things will happen!

Chapter Six
The Energy is Real!

U p to this point we have talked a lot about this energy that exists throughout the universe, but where does this energy come from? It turns out that all energy now in existence was created at the beginning of time and space, as we know it—and it can be mathematically traced back to exact point of creation. Bear with me for a moment on the scientific end of things, and let's take a journey back to the "Big Bang"—the *proven* scientific explanation of the beginning of time-space and all matter that now exists....

When the Universe was created, some thirteen billion (13.7) years ago, scientific evidence and observations have shown that there existed what is referred to as a "singularity;" a very dense ball plasma—of *energy* made up of billions of very tiny fundamental particles known as fermions and bosons. Consider that this very dense ball of energy was held together by a very powerful attractive force (the strong force), which resulted in an infinite density, infinite temperature state of energy that existed at a finite time. This dense ball of energy is referred to as a "singularity."

But where did this dense ball of matter (energy) come from? Here's a highly simplified explanation. Many theories suggest that it was the product of a super energy force that attracted positively and negatively charged particles (particle-anti-particle pairs), pulling them into its energy field. As the opposing poles of various adjoining particles attracted each other ever closer together, the attractive energy force at the center of it all was continuously drawing more and more particles towards its core, continuously increasing both its density and temperature. As this process played out over many hundreds of thousands of years the density of the particles (and therefore the density of *energy*) increased significantly. This compression process continued until the density of these hundreds of billions of particles became very, very tight, resulting in this singularity; the size of which was a small point of energy no larger than the size of a single hydrogen atom! At the beginning of this whole process the attraction and repulsion forces of the particles were balanced, but as the particles became more tightly packed, over time the combined mass of the particles increased, and along with it the gravitational attraction forces. At a finite point in time-space the balance between the particle-anti-particle pairs reached a tipping point. Eventually they got so close together that the "like" poles were now *too* close and *repulsion* forces of the particles suddenly dominated. In an instant; a flash of light—they all repelled each other in one mighty explosion; coined the "Big Bang!"

This explosion of matter—*of energy*—was the beginning of the Universe; the beginning of Space and Time. In the fractions of a second that followed, the expansion of particles (a byproduct of the explosion) slowed and cooled, as they did so, they began to combine together with other energy particles to form what we now know of as atoms, and in the early seconds following this "Big Bang" all of the elements that now exist were created. During the compression process that led up to this explosion of energy, the closer the particles got to one another, the hotter they got. At the very moment of the "Big Bang", the particles together reached temperatures of over a hundred billion degrees, and at these temperatures, the particle speeds during the explosion were "superluminal"—*faster than the speed of light.* When the fundamental particles expanded outward at this tremendous speed (and temperature)—they interacted with other particles and other energy, cooling as they slowed down. In this simplistic manner, all matter that now exists was created; including the planets, our solar system, and millions of other galaxies.[4]

The "Big Bang" was originally theorized by famous physicist George Le Maitre, amongst others, and was later validated by a number of physicists including Dr. Stephen Hawking. They have since proven that everything that exists throughout the entire universe was created from this one singularity and this massive explosion—and that *all of this energy is still connected.* This connection is believed to be the result of what is known as the "Higgs field," a lattice of energy that existed at the very beginning of time-space and now spreads throughout the universe, connecting all matter (energy) within it. *All* of the energy that now exists in the Universe was created in that very instant, that "flash of light" all those billions of years ago.

The energy that exists within each one of us, the energy that is connected through each of us, connected throughout nature, and indeed across the universe; *is this same energy!* How can we be this same energy that was created so long ago and why is this important? Well, scientific research has proven that *energy never dies or goes away… it only changes from one form to another.* Because of this fact, we are inherently connected to the original source energy that created the universe in its entirety! At a very basic (subatomic) level, this is the very same energy that we project with our thoughts, attitudes and intentions.

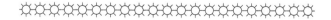

Here's another way to look at the "Big Bang" and the creation of the universe… using the analogy of magnets. We've all seen in science class how the attraction and repelling properties of the opposite poles of a magnet work. We know that the opposite poles attract each other and the like poles repel each other, right? We may also remember that atoms are made up of electrons that orbit a nucleus, and this nucleus is made up of protons and neutrons. Now, if we penetrate deeper into the subatomic structure, we will find that not only are the electrons made up of pure energy, but so are the protons and neutrons, and this energy just happens to be "polarized" energy; with attraction and repulsion properties similar to the positive and negative poles of a magnet. This polarized energy exists as small bundles (particle anti-particle pairs) that make up the very essence of the atom with very strong forces (there are actually four different types, strong, weak, electromagnetic, and gravitational) holding all of these subatomic particles together to form atoms—and the same holds true for multiple atoms that combine to form molecules (and even the planets that form our solar system.) So, if we put all of this energy together, and confine it to a very small space, we will see the attracting and repelling forces of these particles begin to dominate. Just like magnets, the closer the "opposite" poles get; the stronger the attraction force. Likewise, the closer the "like" poles get; the stronger they repel each other. Within each atom all of these forces are balanced. As more and more particles are attracted together in a very small space, the density (and temperature) of particles (energy) increases, and the forces that combine them together become stronger.

These types of attracting and repelling forces are the same forces that were in play during the creation of the universe.

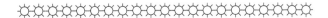

What scientists and physicists of this century have discovered is that our galaxy, like all galaxies across the universe, is *still* expanding. Physicists Penrose and Hawking, among others, theorized that not only the galaxies, but the universe itself is continuously expanding; *still connected by the energy that existed at the time of the "Big Bang."* This is important to note because this fact underlies the concept that we are *all* connected by this same energy. It sounds like a chapter out of some science fiction novel, but it's not science fiction at all—it is actually science fact. The proof exists. Early in 2001 scientists launched a satellite, the Wilkenson Microwave Anisotropy Probe (WMAP)[12] to literally measure the remnant radiant heat (the temperatures) across the universe that resulted from the "Big Bang" explosion. The theory they set out to prove was that the furthest reaches of the universe would be the coolest, and they were right. The mission for the WMAP satellite was to photograph the thermal signatures of our universe and what they found was astonishing.[13] In 2003, with all of this data collected, scientists were able to map the positions and temperatures of all the galaxies, stars and planets across the universe. They not only determined that they were correct in assuming that the outermost reaches of the universe were the coolest, but they also showed that each galaxy was *still expanding outward.* Scientists were able to back trace the moving path of each galaxy (and its temperature) to a single point, *the point in space and time when the universe was created.* The heat signatures (also measured at various different times) showed that each galaxy was also *still cooling,* and this cooling rate could also be traced back to the temperature of our universe at the time of its creation. *So, everything in the universe is still connected, still expanding and still cooling from the massive explosion that took place so many billions of years ago!* Together, these facts born from decades of scientific research provide further proof of our connection to all other matter (and all energy) to the point in time and space when our universe was created, some thirteen billion years ago.

Bringing our discussion back from the very large to the very small; our knowledge of our world grows as our scientific technology becomes more sophisticated. We are now able to probe more deeply and broadly into the mysteries of the atom and its subatomic structure than ever before. The more questions we ask about the scientific basis of all energy; the closer we come to understanding the forces that exist across the universe. We are literally standing on the edge of a great awakening; an emerging global awareness that will be precipitated by the scientific discoveries that we will make in the next few decades ahead. I believe these discoveries will help us to transcend our differences across cultures, languages, and countries and ultimately to bring us closer together as a human race.

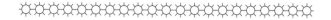

In the last fifty years physicists around the world have made major discoveries in the world of quantum physics. Their discoveries have led to a deeper understanding of the structure of the atom, and of *all* matter and energy that exists throughout the universe. Many of these recent discoveries are being compared to the insights, perceptions, and conclusions that metaphysicians and philosophers have developed over the last twenty-five hundred years. The differences between these two previously disparate paradigms of thought; those of science and spirituality (philosophy) are quickly diminishing. Our scientific concepts of the universe and our technical descriptions of a super energy force that exists are surprisingly similar to descriptions of what so many religions refer to as "God."

At the core of all great religions there are truths and similarities. According to the Bible, God's first command was "Let there be light." (Genesis 1:1-3) Now, light in its most basic form *is* energy. So, let's extrapolate for a moment…. God's first creation was light, and light *is* energy. This seems to coincide with the scientific "Big Bang" Theory we just discussed, which states that all of creation began with a single spectacular burst of light and energy—creating all that exists. They both seem to be saying this: Everything came from this one thing—from this ultimate source of power, energy, light and ultimately life. This original source of light or energy is present within everyone and everything. It is part of who we are and it is where we come from. It connects us all. It is interesting that the Bible tells us that we are "children of God," and that "God is everywhere." This too, makes sense with the scientific facts of the universe and creation we now know to be true. This original "source energy" did give birth to us in a sense—it is where we came from, it is present in all of us and it is all around us; everywhere. Again, science and religion (the Bible in this case) are essentially saying the same thing. The conclusions of modern science and Eastern philosophy are even more consistently parallel. This energy that comprises all that exists is real and it is instantaneously connected across the universe. Could it be that this purest form of energy, which is at the core of all atomic structure, is indeed what many religions may refer to as God? Consider this concept for a moment… because we will come back to this concept later.

For mystics and philosophers the focus of their study is the *inner* world of mind, body, and spirit. Physics, on the other hand, is the study of the *external* world of physical phenomena, and quantum physics in particular is the study of the structure of the atom and its subatomic particles that make up our external world. Scientists base their conclusions on theory, proven through experimentation, while philosophers seem to base their conclusions on experience and observations. On the surface it would certainly appear that these two different disciplines of study are going in opposite directions… but in recent years they have converged.

Over the years I have studied and researched hundreds of books on Eastern and Western religions, as well as the teachings of the ancient Eastern mystics, along with the work of just as many scientists, biologists, psychologists, engineers, and physicists throughout the world. I've always felt a deep need to reconcile the scientific facts with the spiritual and religious side of things and it has been a personal quest for me to do so in order to really understand my own journey through life. I already knew from my own experiences that we were capable of doing amazing things with the power of our minds, but I needed a deeper understanding of how and why this worked. Intuitively, I knew that I would find my answers somewhere between science and religion. I expected to discover a great chasm between the two, and thought I would find widely conflicting perspectives on life and creation between the scientific and spiritual communities; on the surface it would certainly appear that way. Along with many others who have researched these different disciplines, I have been completely amazed by the similarity of conclusions and the parallels that exist between these two distinct schools of thought.

I found that the conclusions of the Eastern mystics, many diverse religions and philosophers along with those of modern physicists and scientists in the last hundred years all point to the same thing: Energy is the starting point for all that exists; it is all that exists; and this energy is connected and networked instantaneously across the universe. It really is amazing. When you strip away all of the rhetoric, the words, the analysis, the opinion, and the hype attached to thousands of years of developed knowledge from all over the world, the conclusion is strikingly simple, undeniable, and direct.

Energy is the essence, the core of all that exists within and across the universe.

We know that the power of the mind (manifested through positive *or* negative thoughts) is translated into an energy field and projected outward into our physical reality. This projected energy in turn attracts people into our lives and stimulates coincidences that either mirror our energy, or provide guidance that is meaningful to us in some way. Our physical reality mirrors the energy we project; it builds with other energy around us to move us father along our life's journey. The world around us mirrors our attitudes and intentions and responds to our expectations. We are what we think. Because this energy across the universe is interconnected across a vast network, each of us is also connected. We are all part of the same whole, and it's fascinating to know that we can trace our own energy and the energy of the universe all the way back to the creation of space and time.

We've used the analogy of the personal energy field that we project expanding throughout our physical reality much like concentric waves expanding outward from a rock tossed into the middle of a calm lake. Just as the waves from the rock reach outward to the far sides of the lake, so too, do our thoughts and intentions reach out across the expanse of the universe. They are manifested in our energy field and they ripple outward to touch the far reaches of our physical reality.

Think of your rock as your thoughts once again. The expanding waves (resulting from the electromagnetic energy that is projected outward) interact with the energy fields of those around you. It turns out that these waves created by the stone you tossed, behave as both a particle and a wave; exactly like the energy of your thoughts. This is a tough concept to grasp, I know, so let me explain: What you see after your rock hits the water is a wave that is created. On a macroscopic (visible) level this wave appears as a continuous outward motion of the water. At the microscopic level, however, each one of the individual water molecules that make up the wave is rotating in a stationary, yet circular motion, with each water molecule exciting (striking) the water molecules adjacent to it. This bumping and excitement continues with all of the water molecules across the entire lake—each molecule hitting the next one, and that one hitting the next one, and so on.... We can't actually see the individual water molecules—we only see the wave, the macroscopic result of the microscopic energy exchange between the molecules. So, you can clearly see that the energy of the wave of water behaves as both a particle *and* a wave. The projected energy from your thoughts behaves exactly the same way!

You're probably wondering why this is important. The energy *we* project, the frequency of energy of our thoughts and intentions interacts with the energy around us just as the water molecules do in the waves on a lake. This is how the electromagnetic energy created by those neurons in our brains can reach out and propagate throughout the world around us. Think of it this way, a Tsunami wave is created and moves across the ocean in the same way that the ripples on a lake are created and reach the far shores. Our energy field excites the very air around us, and in turn propagates outward; similarly affecting the people and the world around us. Our energy also behaves as both a particle and a wave. We sometimes sense or feel the macroscopic results, completely unaware of what is occurring at the microscopic, subatomic level. Because our waves of energy are not "visible" like those created by the rock—we need to consciously remember that we are always projecting some kind of energy, either positive or negative.

In any given moment you *are* that rock—you are *always* sending out some kind of energy ripple out into the world. This is why the concept of the "law of attraction" (which has gained so much notoriety in recent years) actually works! This energy, which is created by our thoughts and feelings, ripples out into the universe interacting with all energy that surrounds us.

Here's the simple scientific explanation that backs this up. Let's go back to the example of magnets we used earlier to explain the attraction and repulsion forces that contributed to the "Big Bang." We are all pretty familiar with magnets—they have "poles" that attract and repel each other. Similarly, *all* particles that make up atoms are also polarized, and therefore all matter is polarized, and so is all energy. So, energy (just like magnets) creates a force of attraction and repelling based on these principals of charged "polar" particles. But in the world of magnets (much like the Earth's magnetic poles) *opposites* attract and likes repel each other.

So the obvious question is this: How does the law of attraction work… if "like polarized energy" doesn't really attract "like polarized energy"… but rather the opposite? At first glance, the science *doesn't* seem to support the concept of the law of attraction—which states that "like attracts like"—in fact on the surface, they seem to completely contradict one another! If you go on the Internet and do a search on the science behind the laws of attraction you'll find a myriad of arm waving and inconclusive articles that all seem to fall far short of scientific explanation. Many motivational books have been written on this subject, but as far as explaining the science behind the scenes—they, too fall short of any thorough scientific explanation, if they even give an explanation at all.

So, bear with me (again) because I will have to fall back on the science to explain. The reality is that *science does indeed support the law of attraction*, but not exactly in the way most people have interpreted it. The law of attraction is in many ways a misnomer—it would be far more accurate to call it the "law of synchronization" or the law of "entrainment." Here is what I mean; first we need to remember that energy has the properties of both a particle (like a marble) and a wave (like the waves on a lake). These properties co-exist together in all particles, and the exact behavior of the particles (meaning whether they behave as either a marble or wave) doesn't manifest until the very instant we observe it. For those of you who are into the science, this is also known as the Heisenberg Uncertainty Principle. The second thing we need to remember is that particles of energy communicate their properties with each other instantaneously; faster than the speed of light (superluminal). These two observations have been both theorized and proven in the laboratory many times dating back to the early 1930's.[14]

What this suggests is that our energy moves through the universe in both a straight line (like a marble) and in all directions (like a wave.) The behavior of this energy as either a wave or particle isn't determined until the very instant we participate or observe it. Therefore, we can conclusively say that *we influence our physical reality just by the act of observing it…* we change our physical reality just by being there! When our energy is "observed" by someone (or something) else in our physical reality the duality of particle properties "collapses" or defaults to a wave function, and these waves ripple across the universe. So far this is only half the answer.

Now, we also know that everything in nature is balanced; the weather, particle/anti-particle forces, the number of positive and negative charges in an atom, Yin and Yang; they are all balanced. When we project energy through our thoughts, attitudes and intentions it is actually a little simplistic to say that we "attract the same kind of energy" from the world around us, but it is easier to grasp when put into this context. We do know that "like" poles of energy repel each other; and this *is* true in the case of a particle, but *not* true in the case of a wave. In the case of a wave; energy behaves differently; it seeks to *synchronize* with energy of similar frequencies. Our thoughts, attitudes and intentions behave in a wave-like manner, not in the manner of a particle (which has polarity). This is why: Our observation of the results (for example, through interactions with other people or events) collapses the particle-wave duality into a wave function. So, our thoughts (energy) possess the properties of a wave as it propagates outward, seeking to "synchronize in frequency" with energy of "like" frequency. The interference phenomenon associated with the wavelike properties of this electromagnetic radiating energy is exactly what gives rise to the *additive properties of similar energy waves*. Once again, this is science fact— proven in the laboratory.[14] What actually occurs during this interaction is a joining of energy frequencies; a *matching* of energy cycles over time (which determines the frequency) that is *complimentary* to the energy we project. We attract energy that "balances and matches" the energy we project; same amplitude, same frequency, in phase. If the two frequencies were placed one on top of the other—they would look the same. Imagine our energy as a puzzle piece—and there is a wavy pattern at the top of this puzzle piece. The energy we attract (or synchronize with) is the *corresponding* puzzle piece whose wavy lines match up with ours. It's not identical, but it is a "match" for our energy. Its patterns (frequencies) match ours. The symbol for Yin and Yang is a good illustration of this; the two sides of the symbol balance and complement each other perfectly. When we correlate this to the law of attraction; the science, at a quantum physics level, *does* indeed support the results.

We haven't changed the laws of physics at all, the opposite poles of the electromagnetic force still behave as they should, but at the subatomic level where we observe the atoms that are made up of these energy bundles all vibrating at specific frequencies, we observe nature at its most fundamental level in its grand balancing act—energy *synchronizing* with like energy. So, to put it in an overly simplistic nutshell; opposites attract when it comes to energy particles, but when it comes to *waves* of energy—like attracts (synchronizes with) like. *This is the science behind the law of attraction.* Through our thoughts and participation in the world around us we are projecting our own energy in *waves*, and the world responds.

So how is it that we are all connected? Why does the energy we project have an effect on people or events around us? As in our previous discussion, all matter is energy, and all energy is connected in a vast network across the galaxies, the universe. In the scientific world, this connection is theorized to be due to the attractive properties of the "Higgs Boson" and more specifically the field that it creates; "the Higgs Field" which is a lattice of energy that extends across the universe.[15] Hence part of the answer comes from the realm of science but we can also look to studies of various religions and mysticism for further confirmation. I am compelled to believe that part of the answer about our connections to the world around us *does* lie in the spiritual realm; in our belief in a supreme being or higher power as well as our connection to this power, and we will discuss these topics in greater depth later on in this book.

For now, though, let's explore the concept of this energy "all around us" a bit more and tie it more closely to how we "see" the world around us. We can't actually see the energy, only its results. Our inner reality, our outer (or physical) reality, and all phenomenon simply exist as different forms of energy: electromagnetic energy that our senses perceive. *Sight, sound, smell, taste and touch, are all forms of electromagnetic energy.* They are detected as different phenomenon by our senses; converted to electrochemical signals and then transmitted through our central nervous system to our brain. Here, the electrical signals are compared with learned patterns and previous experiences and translated into sensations that our brains interpret. "Meaning" is derived by placing the sensations of our physical reality into context through a mapping of our sensations to our experiences. Basically, what we sense with our five senses has to be put into some *frame of reference* in order to gain meaning! If we can't see, smell, taste, hear or touch something, then we will likely not be aware of its existence. If we have never experienced or learned about something, then it becomes much more difficult to put it into that frame of reference or to really "understand" it. Imagine for a moment how the world appears to an infant. An infant can certainly sense the *energy* behind certain things—like the smile of its mother, but this "sensing" is done beyond the realm of the physical world of the five senses. For a baby, the world is just *full* of wondrous and unknown things on the physical or external level; sounds, smells, sights, tastes, and textures—but an infant has yet to form a frame of reference for all of these physical sensations in order to derive meaning. A baby does not know what a flower is, or a rock or a dog, but it seeks to experience these things in every way possible. Everything gets smelled, touched and tasted in a baby's world. We all learn experientially and through this experience we continue the learning process, just like the baby eventually gains the ability to attach meaning (and emotions) to the various physical experiences it has. It learns what certain sounds and words mean, it learns what certain things look like, feel like and smell like—and it defines them according to its life experience thus far. We continue this experiential learning process throughout our entire lives.

Remember our discussion of the macroscopic waves and microscopic water particles when we tossed our rock into the calm lake? You can see the wave but what you cannot see is that the creation of the wave is the result of the energy of the water molecules. *Energy exists all around us, you just can't always "see" it, touch it, smell it, taste it or feel it.* While we have all had glimpses of "sensing" or "knowing" things beyond our five senses, we have (as a species) not really developed our "sixth" sense—which I believe is our *sense of connection* to all that exists. It is not just a function of the physical body we inhabit; it is our intuition, our energy, our life force. It is our awareness of our connection to all that exists, and it lives in our subconscious minds, well beyond the limitations and restrictions of our physical bodies.

Our five senses are limited and we have discovered that many things are not as they might initially appear. So, there are times when our learning and experience have to be rethought. For instance, we now know that solid matter, like the kitchen table or this computer keyboard that I'm typing on, is not solid at all but rather a complex network of energy in motion, just like the water molecules in the wave. Solid matter exists as a collection of molecules: made up of tiny atoms, which are comprised of a nucleus of protons and neutrons, with electrons orbiting the nucleus. In our old high school physics classes we were taught that these were particles (much like marbles) only to learn later through the help of quantum physics that these very particles are actually small energy bundles that possess the properties of both particles and waves. Therefore, everything you think of as a "solid" matter is really just energy vibrating at a different speed or frequency and it only *appears* solid to our limited "five senses."

On a subatomic level it is simply energy in motion—vibrating at a speed and frequency that we are unable to detect with our limited senses. Take our sense of hearing for example: There are frequencies that are too low and too high for us to detect—but they certainly do exist. Consider sound waves (sonic frequencies) for a moment. We are all familiar with the ultrasound; sound waves that are transmitted at such a low frequency that we cannot hear them, but we use them to penetrate matter and provide us with images, like the ultrasound tests that are used to view a fetus in its mother's womb. On the other end of the spectrum is hypersonic sound—like that of a dog whistle—*we* cannot hear it, but it does exists, and a dog certainly *can* hear it. There are many energy frequencies that are simply beyond our range of sensory perception. All energy behaves this same way… it represents a very specific frequency that we can measure in the laboratory.

My point is that just because we don't see or sense something doesn't mean it doesn't exist or hasn't happened. If our senses aren't tuned to detect a change in state of the energy around us or if we don't have the proper symbols or experience to place the experience into context or give it meaning, then we may remain oblivious to an event or occurrence that could be meaningful. Again, this goes back to coincidence and synchronicity in our lives. We may subconsciously sense (through our sixth sense or sense of connection) something powerful in an event or chance meeting with someone, but be consciously unaware of it or oblivious to it. As we discussed earlier—awareness is something we must cultivate in order to strengthen our sense of connection. Our minds are continually filled with conflicting noise and distraction, and we often miss opportunities that present themselves in the form of coincidence.

The scientific explanation is that we perceive the world around us through interpretation of the electromagnetic information detected by our senses. Remember, this sensory information is translated into symbols based upon our acquired memories and placed into context and meaning based upon our experiences and knowledge. This contextual sensory information serves as the foundation for our thoughts and thus interpreted as meaning. These meaningful thoughts and intentions are the force behind the energy we project and to a large degree—they create the reality that we experience.

Say you were bitten by a dog as a child and traumatized by the experience; your sensory experience was painful and fearful—so you would tend to associate dogs with pain and fear… and your thoughts about dogs would be based upon this foundation. If you were to have a later unexpected encounter with a dog you would probably have a visceral reaction of fear and distrust (based upon your prior contextual experience) changing your heart rate and blood chemistry and thereby projecting negative fear based thoughts and energy out into the universe. Your personal experiences create the context and frame of reference for all things—in this case for "dogs" and how you perceive them. If someone else has only had pleasant experiences with dogs (as I have) then their perception and response to this sort of situation would be entirely different, and so would the type of energy they respond with when dogs are present.

Ultimately, our individual consciousness lies at the heart of all that we perceive and experience, all that we think, and all that we are. We cannot really separate our perceptions from our consciousness at all. It is what separates us from other living organic and inorganic matter. In fact, it is our very consciousness and ability to think and reason that has allowed the human race (an otherwise weak species in many ways) to survive not only our more primitive predators but to survive the massive changes in our environment over the millennia.

When we observe the subatomic realm we go *beyond* our experiences and logic, just as we do when we operate with our sixth sense—beyond the realm of the familiar. In both cases we are venturing into a brave new world and we must therefore create a new language, with new symbols and logic in order to try to explain our observations and experiences to others. Interestingly enough, this also holds true when discussing or explaining the experiences of Eastern mystics when they are in a state of enlightenment; at one with the energy of the universe. As Capra suggests in his book, *The Tao of Physics*, both quantum physicists and Eastern mystics will agree that the words and symbols they have to describe their experiences (or their observations) fall far short of being accurate. This is because we simply don't have adequate language or common experiences to put observations into context. Without direct personal experience it is difficult to convey or to understand and words alone are not sufficient.[9]

So, what we take to be true is what we perceive to be our reality, and what we believe to be true is based upon our personal experiences and our perceptions of this physical reality. Our perceived reality is also, in part, shaped by what we expect and *look* for. We have a tendency to believe that what we can *see* is what is true and real. But, again our perception of reality can be misleading, limited to the extent of our knowledge and symbols we have from our life experiences. Let me put this into an imaginary context: Say you meet a caveman that has only seen fire created by rubbing two sticks together, and you show him a lighter that can create fire with the flick of a button. His lack of experience and lack of symbols or words to describe what he sees will surely result in an inability to grasp the concept that the fire from the lighter was created in any other way other than magic or some sort of divine intervention! The lighter is something beyond both the realm of his experience *and* his ability to describe it.

The famous Tai Ji Master, Al Huang, once said "It's easy for me to say and so hard for me to get to you… sooner or later we reach a dead end when we talk."[16] What I interpret this to mean, is that sooner or later we reach a point where words that we know are simply inadequate to describe an experience to someone else. We become limited in our ability to share or convey the experience because our language lacks the terminology to provide an accurate description. Many Eastern mystics have spent their lifetimes practicing meditation and they have been able to move beyond the limitations of the mind and the limitations of experience and symbols. In many verifiable cases they have reached "nirvana," a state of supreme enlightenment where the mind has achieved a oneness with the universe and all that is contained within it. It is said that in this state, they are able to transcend both space and time; "riding along the flow of energy that moves freely throughout the universe." They have, in many cases, spent years training their minds, and senses to become increasingly aware of the energy all around them.[9]

The quantum physics community is now moving in the very same direction, despite their previous conclusions to the contrary. As their instrumentation, particle accelerator technology and power increases—it is steadily leading them closer to the higher energy collisions which are necessary in the study of the subatomic world at deeper levels. Quantum physicists are exploring the subatomic realm far beyond the limitations of symbols and experience in their own right, increasing their own state of awareness, and offering not only a validation of the interconnectedness of the separate parts of the universe, but also of the flow of energy that moves freely and instantaneously throughout the universe. Much like the Eastern mystics, they too have spent years training their minds, and senses (aided by advanced technology) to discover this energy all around them.

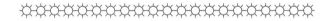

The fact is that *all living organisms are comprised of a complex network of energy.* Our brains are made up of billions and billions of neurons, more than 100 billion brain cells, all connected in a vast network wired across the two hemispheres of our brain. Each of these neurons generates an electrochemical energy that instantaneously passes across the synapses connecting these neurons together. All of our memories, experiences, and all that we have processed with our senses throughout our entire conscious lives, are stored in the contents of this network of neurons: everything we have ever known, thought, felt, tasted, seen, heard or experienced, it's all there! *The electrical energy created by the millions of neurons firing synchronously in our brains creates a measurable electromagnetic* (energy) *field that is projected outward.* This field, the essence of our consciousness, is shaped by our thoughts, attitudes and intentions.

Dr. McFadden, at the University of Surrey in England suggests in his electromagnetic field theory of consciousness (CEMI theory), that the millions of neurons distributed throughout the human brain are unified into a single conscious experience, and thus through the synchronous firing of millions of these neurons, an "endogenous electromagnetic field" is generated by the human brain that embodies our thoughts and intentions. "The human brain's electromagnetic information field is the physical substrate of our conscious awareness—the CEMI field."[2] This electromagnetic (energy) field can be physically measured and is projected outward instantaneously connecting to other energy bundles in our exterior physical world. More specifically, this electromagnetic field couples (synchronizes) with the fields generated by other people, as well as with other matter that exists within our physical reality. As I explained earlier, we entrain the "like" energy of those around us. This concept gives rise to our perceived connections to other people and events in our lives. The electromagnetic field we project couples (synchronizes) with the other fields around us and through this coupling, we are able to influence and affect our physical reality. For example, an Electroencephalography (EEG) test—once popular for detecting abnormalities or tumors in the brain, is the recording of electrical activity along the surface of the scalp that is produced by the firing of neurons within our brain. In the clinical context, EEG refers to the recording of the brain's spontaneous electrical activity over a short period of time. The EEG validates the projection capacity of this energy from our brains. It measures the output of this energy field that is projected from the human brain, created by the synchronous firing of neurons within. This electrical field created at the quantum level between the neurons in our brain *does* exist and it is indeed measurable.

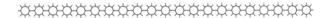

Quantum physics can be pretty intimidating, but here it is in a nutshell. "Quanta" are simply units of light or energy that vibrate at a specific frequency. "Quantum" is energy in motion, so putting these two pieces together; quantum physics is the study of this energy in motion. The quantum physicist's world is the world of subatomic particles. Again, the deeper we explore the structure and makeup of the subatomic particles the more we come to learn that the atom, made up of protons, neutrons, and electrons are really just tiny bundles of energy, constantly in motion that vibrate at specific frequencies. Different numbers of electrons and protons comprise the 117 elements in our periodic table, each of which represent a single type of atom (remember your high school science class?) and they each represent different energy levels; therefore they vibrate at different frequencies. Each atom has its own unique vibrational frequency; just like each of us have our own unique vibrational frequency. With the help of vastly advanced technology quantum physicists have discovered the existence of hundreds of fundamental particles, or energy bundles that make up all atoms. They have also learned that there are four primary forces—different forms of energy, binding these particles (or energy bundles) together within the atom. These forces are: The strong force, weak force, electromagnetic force, and gravity force. Surprisingly enough, gravity is the *weakest* of all of these forces! Depending on which particle we are analyzing, and how deep we go into the realm of the subatomic structure, different forces are at work. What's most interesting here is that these very forces and fundamental particles were present at the beginning of time, and were present in the events of the "Big Bang" that created our Universe and all matter that exists in it.

David Finkelstein, in his paper "Beneath Time, Explorations in Quantum Topology," explained that "the basic unit of the universe was an event, a process that resulted from the collapse of a super dense collection of matter." According to Finkelstein, this super explosion that created the universe and ultimately all energy that exists across the universe did not exist in space and time as we know it, but rather it "existed *prior* to space and time." He goes on to describe space, time, and all matter that exists now as "secondary effects, as byproducts so to speak, of this massive explosion that created the universe." Finkelstein explains that "the basic processes, the ever expanding propagation of energy throughout the universe, is linked together to form local webs, and that smaller webs of energy are further linked into a larger network to create a coherent super position of energy across the universe."[17] The World Wide Web (the Internet) is a pretty great illustration of the concept of a vast interconnected network that you can probably relate to. As new interactions within this universal web of energy occur, as in the collision of subatomic particles or even in the case of two people meeting online through Facebook; in both instances new connections are made; forming a broader network. As each new network connection is made, the "new" particle/energy network embodies the properties of the "old" particle/energy network. This helps to explain why positive (or negative) entrainment of energy breeds more energy of the same type.

Our brains work in much the same way. These networks of electrical connections are very similar in function to the neuronal connections in our brains. *As we develop new experiences, and learn new things we make new connections, we are increasing the expanse of networks in our brains and thus increasing the energy flow and the projection strength of our energy!* The more neurons we have firing synchronously the stronger the energy, and therefore the stronger the projection of that energy into our external world. This is a huge concept, and a really important one to grasp. As we experience, learn and grow throughout our lives, we create these new connections, and they in turn enhance the energy we project—in effect, the more we learn the stronger and more powerful our energy becomes and our ability to impact the world around us increases. This has vast implications and emphasizes the importance of education, diversity and continuous growth on both an intellectual and spiritual level—for us as individuals and as a global community. The more we learn and experience, the greater impact we will have on our own lives and the lives of those around us.

As our awareness, knowledge and experiences increase throughout the scientific, philosophical, biological and psychological disciplines, we as a human race are quickly gaining insight into the potential powers of the human mind to shape and mold our physical realities, manifest coincidences and allow us to change our biological realities and heal ourselves… and even to change the world! Humanity is moving toward a new stage of global co-operation and potentially to a new stage of evolution. Our powerful capacity to change, not only to change ourselves, but to change the direction of our lives and the world around us, lies relatively untapped and dormant within each of us.

If we are to become fully aware, and enlightened enough to use the full potential and power of the mind, then we must continue to build new networks, both within our own minds and across the human race as a whole. We can do this by increasing our knowledge and understanding of our external physical world and by exploring the realm of our own consciousness. The best place to start is through increased self-awareness. Moving beyond that, we must develop a new awareness beyond our senses; develop our "sense of connection." By creating new symbols for our observations and building new experiences, we will be able to "see" with greater insight. As we continue to grow, expand our experiences, and create positive energy along our life journey, we *are* building these new connections. Not only are we expanding the network of connections in our own brains and consciousness, but we are also expanding the network connections with the physical world around us. This expansion will lead us to see the world in a different way. We will have a greater connection to the people around us and we will enhance the overall quality of our lives. In order for this to occur we must *retrain* our thought patterns, open ourselves to greater awareness, to opportunities and new experiences. We must see the world around us as a reflection of ourselves, our attitudes and beliefs. We must also see ourselves and the world around us as part of a unified whole—what we do, what we think, and how we interact within our world affects not only us—but all of those around us.

As the scientific community continues its exploration of our physical world, we must also begin our own inner explorations, and while each of us pursues a journey of introspection, seeking to learn our own value and purpose; mankind moves progressively forward towards a convergence in global awareness. Our progress will be the culmination of both scientific and philosophical experience, and the catalyst for this progress *is* the expansion of our individual awareness.

Now let's bring the concepts of science, energy and human consciousness (awareness) together. Remember, the goal of science and that of scientists is to explore our external environment, the relationships between the elements of our physical world, their behavior, and the properties of cause and effect. What we learn helps us to understand our physical world and our relationship to that world, as well as the confines and constraints that we must accommodate to survive and prosper. In their book, *Mind-Reach*, Harold Puthoff and Russell Targ discuss the convergence of quantum physics with philosophy and human perception. They suggest that "What we experience is *not* external reality at all but rather our *interaction* with it."[18] The physical world, according to quantum mechanics is "not a structure built of existing un-analyzable entities, but rather a web of relationships between the elements whose meaning and purpose arise wholly from their relationships to the whole system," says Capra. "That which connects all matter together in the universe is an undeniable energy force, it moves around us, it moves through us, connects us as elements of a unified whole, and becomes the very matter that we are made of."[9]

Einstein also records a similar observation, "What we perceive as solid matter is nothing more that empty space filled with a pattern of energy running through it."[14] Quantum theory backs up what these renowned physicists observe. As we look at the patterns of energy at the subatomic level we no longer see what were once considered to be elementary particles, we see energy in constant motion and vibrating at well defined frequencies. As Bell theorized, "This energy that makes up all matter oscillates back and forth as pure rhythmic energy. It is the properties of these particles as pure energy that also interlinks all forms of energy instantaneously together across the universe; it is what links all of us as a human race together." He also says, "There is an instantaneous non-local connection between all subatomic particles (energy bundles) that leads to an interconnection of all matter, both organic and inorganic."[19,20] These are the undeniable scientific principles that serve as the foundation and validation for the fact that we are all connected by this common energy force.

Our observation of the world, and indeed, our very existence, changes the world around us. Not only does the energy we project influence others and affect our own physical reality, but the very *act* of our observing and participating, influences the reality of what we perceive at the very moment we view it. Again, this is a result of our energy interacting with the energy all around us. The famous physicist Werner Heisenberg theorized that "The very observations or measurements we make of our physical reality will change the outcomes of our observations or measurements."[21] What he concludes is that we influence the outcome of an event or interaction by the very fact that we are observing or measuring it, a theory known as the Heisenberg Uncertainty Principal. So, once again—the electromagnetic energy field that we project, the product of our consciousness, interacts with our physical world and through this interaction bends it or shapes it according to our thoughts and intentions. We co-create our own reality!

How we see and perceive the energy around us depends entirely on our state of mind. In the scientific community it is believed that the very attitudes and intentions of the observer influence the outcome of the experiment; the measurements, and even the observed results. Both Capra and Zukav's conclusions are consistent with the Heisenberg uncertainty principal: These bundles of energy—those which are the subject of the experiment react to our observations and bend in response to our intentions and thoughts! Not a concept, not a myth—but a proven scientific fact. "Given that the basic make up of the universe is pure energy that is instantaneously connected to the whole; this energy and the network of this energy is malleable to human intentions and thoughts, conforming not just to our expectations but transforming to align with the very frequency of energy that we project."[22]

These conclusions validate my own experiences. We can heal our bodies with the power and energy of our minds, with our positive thoughts and attitudes. We can change our physical reality, and mold it to conform to our expectations and intentions. Our thoughts, expectations and intentions flow out into our physical world and the world will mirror and respond to this very energy. We are what we think, and the world is as we expect it to be. Our physical reality conforms to our expectations. *Are you seeing the importance of positive thoughts and intentions here?*

Again, this is science fact not science fiction. This capacity we have to influence each other and change our physical reality has been validated in the scientific community time and again. Furthermore, these very facts correspond quite closely to nearly twenty-five hundred years of human observation, wisdom and experience documented by the ancient Eastern philosophers. As Gary Zukav states in his book, *The Dancing Wu Li Masters*, "Western science is coalescing with the higher dimensions of human experience. The study of Eastern philosophies shows that a profound and penetrating intellectual quest into the ultimate nature of reality can and does set the stage for a quantum leap beyond what we see as our physical reality."[22]

We have still not quite closed the gap completely between science, Eastern philosophy, and human consciousness, but we are getting closer every day. It is believed that we are very close to discovering the elusive "connector" energy (the Higgs Boson or "God" particle) the super "connective" force that is responsible for the superluminal communications of all energy. Through CERN we may find the answers to our questions. When we reach this point in the scientific realm, our wisdom of the world will take one giant step forward. Our knowledge of these particle interactions will grow and we will be one step closer to a final validation of the interconnectedness of all energy in the universe. At that point in time the quantum physicists will have reached their own state of enlightenment—through their research and experimentation, much like the ancient mystics who have reached a similar state through meditation and introspection. It's an interesting juxtaposition: One group exploring our external physical reality, the other group exploring our internal spiritual reality. Two completely different paradigms, two completely different journeys, both arriving at the same conclusion: We are all interconnected across a vast network of energy.

This energy exists, it's always been there, and it is all around us. This energy connects *all matter* that exists together into a unified whole. Nature and the ecosystem we live in are a critical part of this unified whole, and all parts of the system are interconnected. When part of the system is sick, all parts of the system lose energy and eventually become sick. We see this occurring everyday in nature, and with what's going on with our global environment. It's also the same thing that's happening to our global economy. When one part of the system gets sick, eventually the whole system gets sick. All networks are like this, and networks are made up of energy. This applies to us as individuals as well: when we catch a cold it starts in our sinuses, moves to our lungs and head, and pretty soon we are flat on our back in bed with the flu. First one person in the family gets it, and then the whole family has it, and so on. This is why worldwide epidemics such as the H1N1 virus are of such great concern. *We really are all part of a single unified whole—our environment, our economy, the human race... everything!*

This energy that connects us all, and the frequency of the energy that we project, is mirrored by the world around us. This is the very same energy that connects all of the various parts of our mental and physical reality together. When I talk about changing the world one person at a time, I am talking about changing the world with the positive energy that we create, that we project with our attitudes, thoughts and intentions. *Change yourself, and you will change the world!*

Chapter Seven
Two Different Journeys,
Same Destination

S o now we have a better understanding of the science behind this energy that lies within each of us and that connects all that exists. But what is the supporting evidence found in the ancient texts and philosophies of the Eastern regions of the world, and what about the other branches of science?

Eastern philosophers have long maintained that we are connected to all that exists across the universe through a common web of energy. Their journey to enlightenment is often characterized as a spiritual journey, a quest for the source of the energy in each of us and in nature. And as we have just discussed in the previous chapter, Quantum physicists and scientists have pursued quite a different path towards the discovery of this energy through explorations of the inner workings of the atom through scientific research aided by ever advancing technology and experimentation. Through their own processes each group has discovered the same truths… we are all made up of this same energy and through this energy we are connected to each other and to everything that exists in the universe. This energy is the common thread that binds us all together, it is the common denominator in the two distinctly different paradigms of thought, and indeed, it is the same endpoint for both of their distinctly different paths to the truth about our origins. Discoveries in quantum physics over the past few decades have exposed the facts of our previous concepts about the origin of the universe, the structure of the atom, and the very fundamental particles that represent the basic origins of all matter. The idea that we (and the very energy we are made of) are separate from either other living organisms or inorganic matter couldn't be farther from the truth. All matter is energy in its most fundamental form— immediately interconnected through a vast network that spans the entire universe.[9]

The past several decades have led to some incredible discoveries in modern physics. Great strides have also been made in cognitive research, and in the areas of neuroscience and psychology that validate the existence of this energy field that is created within our very consciousness. Arne Naess, the Norwegian philosopher and expert on deep ecology says, "The world is not made up of a collection of isolated objects but rather is a network of phenomena that are interconnected and interdependent." He goes on to say "All that exists is connected to nature, connected to the universe and connected to a higher power."[23] Adding to this concept, Biologists Humberto Maturana and Francisco Varela, in their Santiago Theory of Cognition state, "The mind is not a thing, but rather a process." The mind (our consciousness) "is a process of cognition which embodies the process of life. Therefore, consciousness is an elaborate form of life's process." Maturana and Varela describe mind and matter as virtually identical, and they go on to say, "The brain and body are the structure through which this process of life manifests itself. Spirit is the breath of life; the very breath of one's soul."[24,25] These same concepts are also communicated repeatedly in philosophical and spiritual traditions throughout the world. Philosophers, scientists and many religious doctrines all seem to offer very similar viewpoints about the network of energy that exists between mind, body, and spirit.

Scientific theories now correlate quite closely with the observations and teachings of the ancient Eastern mystics and philosophers that were initially set forth over 2,500 years ago. They too declared the existence of a universal energy present within each of us, believing that this energy existed at the core of all living creatures, and that this energy was somehow connected to all life that exists in nature. Moreover, these ancient philosophers went on to suggest that we could influence our physical reality through the sheer force of our will and intentions. Sounds familiar, doesn't it? With the recent advances in science we find ourselves in the midst of an unprecedented convergence of these different paradigms of thought about the human experience, the universe, and our very participation in creating our own physical reality.

No doubt there have been times when you have felt your own deep connection of mind, body, and spirit to the vast universe. How can you help but feel a sense of awe and wonder when you gaze at the evening stars on a clear quiet night? Even more awe inspiring is the knowledge that we are *one* with the heavens above; we may be tiny specks within this vast universe, but we are an integral part of the whole; we are connected to it all!

Within the texts and philosophies of the Eastern regions of the world lies great wisdom, and it is there that their conclusions to life's challenges and questions are contained. Their conclusions are subjective by nature; they are conclusions based on introspection, observations and the combined experiences of a broad collection of philosophers, mystics, and prophets amassed over thousands of years and across several different continents and cultures. Given their very different methods of validation (observations versus experimentation), the likelihood of their conclusions being similar with those of the western scientists, seems slim, but it is indeed the case! The Eastern regions of the world have remained quite consistent in their observations and teachings for several millennia. By comparison, the scientific community has undergone radical changes in concepts and theories—especially over the last several hundred years, with the most recent breakthroughs in physics and quantum physics occurring in just this past century. These most recent revelations in just this decade alone have scientists finally converging on a "Unified Theory of Everything," a theory that promises to show us scientific proof of how all the pieces of life and energy are connected together across the universe. As Capra suggests "The two foundations of modern 20th century physics, namely quantum physics and Relativity Theory, both force us to see the world very much in the same way a Hindu, Buddhist, or Taoist sees it, and these similarities become more profound as we explore the phenomena of subatomic (microscopic) particles of which all matter is made."[9]

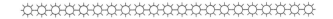

So, how did this division between science and philosophy originate, and how did we get to the point where East and West seemed to move in such polar opposite directions? History shows that there was a great split between philosophers and scientists of the Western world that occurred during the time when the Greeks ruled the scientific community. There were numerous contributing factors to the gradual split between science and philosophy (including politics and religious doctrine) and this split was reinforced by the notion of duality in nature; the concept that two parts necessarily make up the whole, like good and evil, heaven and earth, day and night. So, during this time in history scientists began to focus their studies on the Earth, the planets, the human body and cause and effect; while the philosophers, particularly in the East, focused their studies on the spirit, the soul, the mind and our consciousness.

As Zukav describes, "this great divide between the scientists and philosophers continued for many centuries eventually leading to two distinctly different paradigms of thought, effectively separated by eastern and western continents."[22] It was an interesting time, filled with widely diverse theories and postulation. In the 16th century, Galileo (believed by many to be the father of science as we know it) combined mathematics with empirical knowledge; knowledge derived from tests, and validated through experiments. Galileo's work also propagated this concept of dualism, which dominated the scientific studies of the time. Famous mathematician René Descartes suggested that our physical reality was driven by two separate and distinct forces, one of mind and one of matter, while Isaac Newton considered matter to be split in two; dead, inorganic matter and living organic matter—each of which, he theorized, were completely separate and distinct. The consensus among scientists of that period was that the Earth was the center of the universe and that mankind (in his infinite wisdom) ruled the Earth and heavens, so therefore man was the true center of the universe. During this same period René Descarte believed that our material world was made up of a multitude of different, separate and independent parts that were "assembled" into a huge machine—a machine that was referred to as the world, and, indeed the universe itself. Newton contributed the mathematical formulas and his own set of immutable laws that governed the way this "huge machine" runs. Together these concepts and laws served as the basis for the "mechanistic" view of the order of nature that would influence the scientific community for the next several hundred years. You get the picture... the original split that occurred between science and philosophy in the western world evolved into a huge chasm during those particular years in history contributing to the division of religions, people, and cultures

At this same time, the Eastern regions of the world were still dominated by a belief in the unity of all things. The Eastern mystics steadfastly believed that we, as a human species, were not ruled by a supreme being with a divine power, but rather that we were all part of the same whole, the same energy force. They asserted that our relationships to one another were part of a process—part of a cycle that ebbed and flowed as a part of the natural order of all that exists balanced between weak and strong (Yin and Yang.) "These philosophers and mystics also believed that the universe was a dynamic cosmos, alive and in constant motion."[7] They believed that everything that exists within the universe, both living and non-living, was made up of the same energy. The foundation of the Eastern religious beliefs aligned with and followed the laws of nature; rooted in the concept of unity and the interrelatedness of all that exists and occurs within a dynamic universe in motion.

The major ideologies that dominated the Eastern and Western cultures at the time *still* serve to dominate these regions—even to this day. While the Western regions continued to be driven further apart by the concepts founded in this separation of mind and spirit, the Eastern regions were drawn closer together—further unified in their beliefs. While the major Eastern religious philosophies such as Hinduism, Buddhism, and Taoism may all differ somewhat in their descriptions of how all living and non-living entities are connected, they all seem to draw similar conclusions about the energy in the universe, the relationships amongst the different parts, and the unifying forces that hold everything in existence together.

The separate and distinct views of the world, driven by the two dominating paradigms of thought in the Eastern and Western countries, led to a fragmentation of mind and spirit, not only in the eyes of the scientists and philosophers, but in the many cultures that dominated these different regions of the world. This fragmentation of mind and spirit eventually started a movement away from the concept of dualism, particularly in the West. While the Eastern cultures seemed to be pulled together by the core of their beliefs, the Western cultures seemed to have been driven farther apart by the many concepts promoted by this dualism. The people in the West were also further separated by the actions of various regional rulers of the time who leveraged the dualism of religious faith with science as a way to control and create different classes of people based upon wealth and power. This continued for hundreds of years, and it is only in recent times—particularly since the advances in physics in this century, that the rift between science and philosophy has begun to heal and close.[9]

Over the course of thousands of years, both the Eastern philosophers and the Western scientists each assimilated their own vast bodies of knowledge through their different types of research. Scientists and physicists have compiled a massive body of empirical data and knowledge about our physical reality, the creation of the universe, and most recently—the subatomic structure and forces of nature. Philosophers and mystics have amassed a similar body of knowledge based upon their insight, observations and intuition in regards to the human species and our physical reality. The combined knowledge from these two independently created bodies of data draw strikingly similar conclusions about the energy source that serves as the foundation for all matter and it's network of connections throughout the universe.

So what can we learn from these two disparate bodies of knowledge and experience that is relevant to our quest for understanding the energy within us all? First of all, there are many paths to the same destination, and while the science took a more circuitous route than philosophy, it is certainly making up for lost time in recent years! Both paradigms are valid and together they provide a truly comprehensive look at how we interact with the world around us. There is much to be learned from both sides and from their uniquely different approaches to seeking knowledge, insight and wisdom.

Western science tends to work in a very structured way; developing knowledge through experience based upon observations of action and reaction (causal) events in our physical reality. In the western world, we create knowledge based connections between these events and reactions within our physical reality using words or symbols that label our experiences, and our thought processes as a result of these observations are therefore linear and logical. By our very nature, we tend to create boundaries and rules about our physical reality based upon this structured thinking. What we have discovered, in the past few generations, however is that the natural world, and therefore our physical reality, is *nonlinear*—not connected in a straight line, not causal at all! *This suggests that our structured thinking can only answer some of our questions when it comes to understanding ourselves and our relationship to the world around us.*

Eastern philosophers and mystics, on the other hand, have always approached their quest for knowledge from a much more personal perspective. Concerned more with gaining understanding through a "more intimate experience" with their reality, they often achieve enlightenment through deep meditation or quiet observations of the world around them. This process has allowed them to transcend the limitations of both intellectual thought and sensory perceptions. Their process is quite the opposite of the western "structured" approach. They use absolute knowledge and personal observations as their basis of their belief structure, achieved only by *escaping* the boundaries of logic, thought, and the linear constructs of one's consciousness. It is this "non-linear" thinking that we must also consider and utilize in order to truly understand our connection to the world around us.

Think about this for a moment... this alignment of Western science and Eastern philosophies is also leading to an amazing re-alignment for humanity!

Both the Western scientist and Eastern philosopher have learned that all that exists is pure energy, networked throughout the universe, and all parts that exist are elements of a single unified whole. They have both discovered independently, and by quite different means, that this energy is often beyond our perception, beyond the ability of our senses to detect or "see." Nonetheless, it is there, it is real, and everything that we observe in our physical reality is a manifestation of this very energy. Whenever we expand the realm of our experience—the limitations of our rational mind as governed by known symbols and words becomes apparent. Seeking to fit these new experiences into our current perceptions of reality simply does not work, and this forces us to abandon many of our old concepts and logic governed by our intellect. In order to process these new experiences we must learn to open our minds, think in a less "linear" fashion, and experience our physical reality from a heightened level of "non-linear" awareness—a new level of consciousness. So, you may be asking yourself "How do we open our minds"?

Capra says, Eastern mystics and philosophers seek intuitive knowledge through meditation and the mystical experience, while Western scientists seek rational knowledge, and yet each knowledge base parallels the other. This parallel is further reinforced by the nature of the mystical experience. It's described in the Eastern traditions as direct insight, which lies outside the realm of intellect. This type of insight is the result of *being* rather than thinking. By looking deep inside" of ourselves instead of just looking at our external physical reality, we can connect with the energy of the universe. There is much to be said for this approach; *all growth and change begins with us, and it all begins by looking within.* "The mystical experience of reality is an essentially non-sensory experience, derived from meditation and deep introspection, a different mode of perception and thought. It is a valuable and effective means of connecting with your subconscious mind. While deep meditation typically serves as the source of these non-sensory experiences of our reality, many of us experience something quite similar that leads us to flashes of insight."[9]

You've probably had these "flashes" of insight at some point yourself, these sudden moments of connection, clarity and understanding. Your subconscious mind is always "open" and processing information, and it typically communicates with your conscious mind via these sudden flashes of insight or intuition—those moments when that light in your brain suddenly goes in an "AHA" moment. I vividly remember this happening back in one of my college graduate classes. I had a really difficult linear algebra class and despite the professor's explanations, I still just wasn't getting it. It didn't click for me at all. It was a few weeks later while sitting in another class altogether (a finite elements structures class where linear algebra concepts were used to solve an applications problem) when suddenly it connected—and I *instantly* got it. It was as though the entire puzzle suddenly came together. I saw how all the math and theory could be used to solve real world problems! Once the light went on in my head, the breadth of applications became profoundly clear and simple. For me, it was a moment of profound insight and clarity... a moment of "enlightenment." These flashes of insight can readily occur for both the mystic *and* the scientist, often leading them to breakthroughs in understanding and knowledge.

Rational knowledge and rational activities constitute the majority of scientific research but scientific researchers will also often rely on their instinct and non-rational thinking to guide their research into new areas of investigation. To some extent they allow their intuition to lead them to new approaches or ideas that ultimately may lead to breakthroughs, and in most instances where groundbreaking discoveries have been made, it has been flashes of insight (derived from their subconscious thoughts) that have led to these great discoveries. Non-linear thinking leads to new awareness, insights, and ultimately to new breakthroughs. Albert Einstein, when asked about the "eureka" moment of discovering the simplicity and directness of the general theory of relativity, once described it this way, "We experience an awakening of the mind and spirit."[14]

Chuang Tzu once said, "The still mind of the sage is a mirror of heaven and Earth, the glass of all things." This "still mind" he describes is something that we can all aspire to. I believe that what he is saying here is that when we project our own attitudes and beliefs we change that which we perceive. The still and quiet mind of a sage projects *no* bias; therefore he perceives the world in a much more pure fashion... as it truly is. A similar connection can be made during meditation wherein we must truly "quiet our inner mind" in order to reach a point of pure separation from our physical world. Zukav, in his book, *The Dancing Wu Li Masters,* says "There is some evidence that consciousness at the most fundamental levels is a quantum process... if we can experience the most fundamental functions of our psyche and if they are quantum in nature then it is possible that the ordinary perceptions of space and time might not apply to them (the ancient mystics) at all."[22]

So why then have the Western scientists been so far behind the Eastern mystics in their search for ultimate wisdom, or more to the point, why so long in getting real answers? Part of the answer lies in the maturity of the technology necessary for us to peer deeper into the subatomic realm. Most notably though is the evolution of physics itself that was needed in order for science to progress to a point where we could see what we were searching for. In the world of physics we have the "old school" physics and the "modern" physics. Both have useful theories that help to explain our physical reality. The old school physics, dominated by the Newton's "mechanistic" model is used for explaining the world around us when the objects we're observing are big, and the speed of these objects are small when compared to the speed of light, such as the case of planets in our solar system, and objects like cars and planes. Modern physics comes into play when these conditions *don't* apply. Modern physics, as described by Einstein's Theory of Relativity Theory for example, come into play when we are investigating the much smaller realm of molecules and atoms, where the speed of the objects were are looking at approach the speed of light. As we probe still deeper into the atomic structure "quantum" physics takes over to help us explain and understand what we observe in the even smaller realm of subatomic particles.

In the Western world, new paradigms of thought in science, particularly in quantum physics, have been somewhat constrained by centuries of structured, linear, rational thinking. We initially tried to impose this structured thinking on what happens in the subatomic realm and we aligned our observations within our existing frame of reference; the fundamental laws we were familiar with that were consistent with the mechanistic, macroscopic world, and sensory perception. But, this structure and logic breaks down quickly when we move past the macroscopic to the microscopic subatomic realm, which lies far beyond our normal senses. Zukav puts it this way, "The deeper we probe the more we must abandon the constraints of our linear thinking that served us well in the macroscopic world but fall far short in explaining our observations of the tiny subatomic physical reality that lie beyond our five senses and vocabulary. We are now taking a cue from the Eastern traditions and using a more cross dimensional, non-linear approach to understanding this subatomic world."[22]

We are all part of a very complex system of interactions, relationships, and events; connected with each other and to our physical reality through a common, networked connection of energy. We are what we think; our conscious and subconscious minds project an energy field that is a manifestation of our thoughts, intentions, and desires and the world around us mirrors the energy we project. The world around us becomes what we expect it to be. Hence, the energy field that we continuously project interacts with our physical reality and the energy fields of people around us. This conclusion offers the scientific explanation for our ability to affect changes in our physical reality as well as our ability to heal ourselves and to influence the people around us. All of this occurs as a direct result of the frequency of our projected energy field interacting with the various energy frequencies it encounters.

Our universe is truly a dynamic and unified whole. As Einstein once said, "We can never separate space and time, but rather that it exists as a continuum."[14] Even our observations affect our realities. The Heisenberg Uncertainty Principle has repeatedly been validated, suggesting that the observed is intrinsically affected by the observer. These theories together tell us that the observer and the observed are connected together in a space-time continuum. The Eastern philosophers have long held that we are all part of a unified whole... and one with nature and mother earth (GAIA.) What does this really mean? It means that we are all connected together via this vast network of energy and that we can (and *do*) influence our physical reality both by observing and participating with the reality that surrounds us, and in the process of nature that occurs within and around us. Once again, these conclusions are strikingly similar to the conclusions originally reached by the Eastern mystics and philosophers over 2500 years ago, and validated by subsequent practitioners of these religions for the centuries ever since then.

Two different journeys, one single common goal and destination: To find the truth behind our reality. The energy is there, it pervades all that exists, and while our senses aren't developed adequately to "see" it directly; we know it is there, we can measure it and we can observe many of the phenomena in our physical reality that result from it. The core theme of the various Eastern religious philosophies is the unity and interconnectedness of everything that exists and occurs in the universe… and the world of science now concurs.

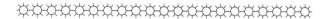

So let's put these science and philosophy pieces together. We observe, we interact, we participate and as a result we directly influence our physical reality. The beginning and end of what happens in our physical reality, as described by either the philosopher or the scientist, always lies in the consciousness of the participant, and energy is the common denominator that binds us all together. *We have now come full circle.*

As Heisenberg states, "What we observe in nature is not nature itself, but rather nature exposed to our questioning, our inquiries, and our observations. We interact with nature and by our very presence we influence directly, that which we observe."[21] In some strange sense the universe is a participatory universe. Mystical knowledge can never be obtained by mere observation of our physical reality; it requires full participation and involvement with the whole being. Capra points out that "The Eastern world view has pushed this notion to the extreme with the belief that the observer and observed, subject and object, are not only inseparable but indistinguishable. This unity and oneness with the universe that both the mystics and physicists alike speak of is achieved purely in the state of consciousness where the individual dissolves in the indistinguishable oneness, when the world of the senses is transcended."[9] Chuang Tzu describes his experience in these words, "My connection with the body and its parts dissolved; my perceptive organs are discarded. Thus leaving my material form and bidding farewell to my knowledge, I am become one with the Great Pervader, this I call sitting and forgetting all things."[27]

In the world of modern physics Einstein, Bohr, Bell, Hawking and others have expanded our insights into the subatomic structure forcing us to abandon the concept that our physical reality is constructed of independent, separate parts, but rather that all parts, made up of energy, are connected and networked as a unified whole. Heisenberg has opened our eyes to the concept that we are not merely observers of our physical reality—but rather *participants.* As Stapp, McFadden and Jung have taught us; our very consciousness may in fact be responsible for our perceptions of our physical reality. In fact, our perceptions may very well be *creating* our reality. We have come to view the universe as an interconnected web of physical and mental (consciousness) relationships whose individual and separate pieces are only defined in the context of the whole they comprise. To the Buddhist, for example, there is no separate external world that he observes, participates with, or inserts his will upon. The Lama Govinda describes this concept of unity beautifully, saying, "The external world and the internal world are two sides of the same fabric within which the threads of all forces, all events and the elements of one's consciousness are woven into, and which together are inseparable from the unity of the universe."[28] The devout Buddhist typically believes that we should strive for transcendence of the world of society and everyday life, in order to reach a higher plane of consciousness, and attain a mystical union with the universe.

This basic unity of the universe is an underlying current that runs as a common denominator within the Eastern philosophies and it is also a common theme in the observations of modern physics. The deeper the quantum physicists probe into the subatomic structure with the help of ever advancing technology, the more they discover the common roots of the energy that exists there. The more we learn, the closer we come to understand that *everything* we observe in our internal and external physical reality is the result of the relationships of this energy at the subatomic level, and in turn at the atomic and molecular level. Everything that we observe is driven by the interconnection and interdependence of the atoms, their subatomic structure and the forces that bind them, and the bundles of energy that form the foundation for all that exists. In the end, the philosophers and scientists may have taken very different paths, but they have shared a common goal; the search for truth and wisdom, and it has led them to the same destination.

Chapter Eight
Balancing the Flow of Our Energy

B y now you understand that the energy we have been discussing is indeed real, and that we really are all connected to each other and the world around us. But how do we apply these concepts in our everyday lives… and why is balancing this same energy in our lives so important?

Human beings are magnificently complicated organisms. Our biological makeup and the function of our organs and bodily systems are incredibly complex, but our brains are the most complex of all; made up of billions upon billions of tiny neurons, all interconnected in a large electrical network. The health and operation of every biological function in our body relies on relatively small tolerances in the balance of the chemical elements that flow through our bloodstream and our circulatory system, bathing each and every one of our cells. We also know that our brain chemistry (which is responsible for the electrical energy that underlies all functions and information transfer within the neurons in our brains) is *very* sensitive to the balance of our blood chemistry. Nature always seeks a balance, and balance is an essential component in *every* aspect of our lives—essential not only for maintaining healthy minds, bodies and spirits, but also for maintaining a healthier world.

As such, each one of us, individually, represents a highly complex web of this connected energy. Adding to the complexity of our *personal* network of energy—we live within a large *social* network where we are continually interacting with others—each of whom are made up of their own complex networks of energy. Beyond that, we also operate on an even larger scale as a *society*, with a myriad variety of cultures, and other species, all of which adds to the complexity of this extremely large network of energy. You get the picture. We are each microcosms of the whole; part of this huge, vastly complex energy network. Nature itself is comprised of a very complicated set of interrelated elements, and each one also has its own unique energy pattern. As human beings we must all work together and find our balance; we must do this collectively on an external level in order to survive as a species on this Earth, and on an internal level as individuals, too. Now, finding our collective balance is tough enough when the entire system is healthy and working properly, but if you throw in the current status of our global economy, a worsening environmental situation, regional conflicts and wars that are being fought in many different nations, and the increasing threat of poverty and famine—it becomes even tougher. We have pretty well stressed out our system, and right now we are completely off balance on a global level. At the very core of all biological and non-biological matter is this vast connected network of energy... and this energy relies on a delicate balance to keep it functioning smoothly, just as our bodies do.

Energy makes up all matter, flowing freely through and within everything that exists, and it is connected instantaneously across the universe. When one part of the system gets sick, eventually the whole system gets sick. This holds true not only for each one of us as individuals, but also for the society we live in and for the human race as a whole, just like the networks we discussed earlier. Part of what is currently making us sick on a global level is the desire for *control*. Wars are continually being waged by nations fighting other nations in order to gain control of natural resources, ideologies, economies, and even for the purpose of controlling and dominating the very people that live there. These conflicts arise out of the desire to "control" the basic energy symbolized by the source of the conflict. As a human race we precipitate these control wars on each other not only as nations, but also as smaller groups, and even as individuals. When you break these conflicts down to the very root cause—whether the conflict is about oil, ideologies, natural resources, or even an argument between spouses; *the very source of the conflict is almost always a desire to control the energy of the other.* During these conflicts, one party is trying to gain control over the source of the other's energy; that's their objective.

There is a finite amount of energy in the universe, and all the energy that now exists originated with the "Big Bang." Because the energy that exists across the universe is a *constant*; the total sum of this energy neither increases nor decreases. It merely changes from one form to another in the pursuit of balance and harmony. Nature is in a never ending cycle of renewal, a process that moves energy through the system as it changes form. This process is happening all around us: the changing of the seasons; day and night; birth and death; the creation and destruction of cells in our bodies. These are all cycles that facilitate the changing forms and renewal of energy in the universe, on the planet Earth, and within each of us. Within nature and the natural order of the universe, there are no conflicts over the control of the flow of this energy; it is simply a natural process of balance and renewal.

The human species is different. We have a highly developed consciousness and we are able to think and reason. We might not always make the best decisions, but this is fundamentally what sets us apart from other species. By our very nature we are pre-wired for survival, and our basic instincts seem to drive us to want to control things—including the energy of those we come in contact with. This is not always deliberate or intentional, but as a species we do have quite a history of conflict; of seeking to aggressively control and capitalize upon the energy of others. In order for us to actively harmonize with nature and the rest of the universe, we need to move past this desire to control everything and everyone within our reach!

The energy flow in nature always seeks to find a balance; a harmony with the energy in the universe. The energy fields that each one of us projects will also, by their very nature, seek to harmonize or synchronize with other similar energy fields. As your energy seeks this balance, barriers can often arise restricting the free flow of energy. Obviously, these are barriers we want to avoid whenever possible. They typically manifest in the form of power struggles or control issues and they obstruct this natural flow. When the energy flow is blocked, synchronization and communication can't occur, balance can't be achieved, the internal balance of energy for each party is thrown into chaos, and negative energy floods the system—resulting in conflict.

So how do you find this balance in your own energy? The answer is rather simple: Stay positive and harmonize with others and the world around you. Give your energy away freely. By giving of your energy freely, (through cooperation for example) you will reach a common frequency and a harmony with the energy of those around you, as well as with your surrounding physical reality. As you do this your energy will increase. Remember the example of the two stones tossed together into the calm lake? The waves got higher as their energy flow was synchronized.

You can manage your own energy by managing your attitude and intentions. Let go of any power struggles that are present in your life, become aware of your own need for control, and learn to minimize or eliminate it; only then will your energy flow freely. As you work through these barriers you will start to see and feel the effects. You will literally feel more alive, more clear, calm and focused. As your internal energy increases, you will automatically attain a higher degree of harmony, a synchronization of your own internal frequency. You will also notice an increased awareness and heightened level of your senses. Coincidences will become more apparent, easily identified, and frequent. The positive effects will begin to compound and the positive energy will build, accelerating you towards your goals and objectives—towards the results you seek.

Here is why this concept of balance (energy balance) is so important: When the flow of energy becomes blocked in one part of the system—a cascading effect occurs where every part of the affected system gets impacted, transforming the energy of the whole into negative energy. Look at our rainforests; through irresponsible and unbalanced harvesting of these areas, we have damaged a part of the system and the repercussions (to name but a few) are the destruction of entire ecosystems, reduction of our ozone layer, and increased global warming, not to mention the cultural impacts for those living within these regions. Everything is connected—and all actions affect the whole.

James Redfield discusses the issues of energy control and what he calls "control dramas" in considerable depth in his book, *The Celestine Vision*. He suggests that the process of psychological domination can be observed everywhere, and it is the underlying source of all irrational conflict in the human world, from the level of individuals all the way to cultures and nations.[29] In order to create more positive energy in our lives, we want to mitigate or minimize conflicts and the flow of negative energy. We can jump start this process by becoming increasingly self-aware and identifying our own power struggles and control issues. As we develop a conscious awareness of the balance and the harmony of this energy within ourselves we also develop an increased awareness of our balance with the energy of those around us.

Someone's desire to control the energy of others is typically an attempt at increasing their own total energy, by taking it from others rather than attempting to reach their own internal balance and building from that. In the energy conflict that ensues, whether you are the "victim" or the "instigator," this type of conflict *always* results in a negative flow of energy. Many people seem to associate "power" with the control of energy, and therefore they seek to gain power over others as a way to control their actions, and sometimes even their thoughts and behaviors.

Interestingly, the flipside of this type of energy domination is an open, free exchange of energy between people, which always results in a net positive increase of energy for everyone involved. It becomes a "win/win" situation. When you give your energy freely to one another, both you *and* the other person gain more energy in return. This is positive, healthy interaction that nourishes uplifts and supports both parties—raising their energy levels and often resulting in a euphoric feeling. It's a lot like the feeling of falling in love; that high that comes from the flood of energy into your system, a result of your frequencies of energy harmonizing beautifully in a free exchange of energy with one another. The positive energy flow that takes place translates to increased endorphin levels in your bloodstream, and millions of neurons in your brain firing synchronously—both of which contribute to this feeling of euphoria. Imagine how different the world would become if we were to stop struggling for control over one another and consistently interact with this mutually cooperative flow of energy on a larger scale... between cultures and countries!

Again, the goal here is to attain a balance of our internal energy. This will lead to a balanced, positive flow of external energy that will, in turn, align with the world around us. We can control the type of energy we project, either positive or negative, through our thoughts and attitudes and we can direct it wherever we want to through our focus. Remember that power struggles, however they are manifested; as individuals, as groups, or countries *always* end up badly for all involved. The net energy exchange in power struggles is always negative—and ultimately no one wins.

Eliminate the power struggles in your life, and distance yourself from those that may attempt to control you, or to control your energy. Look at yourself and your relationships objectively and see if these questions apply in your life: Are you a victim or an instigator of these control activities in your own relationships? Consider how you interact with members of your family, friends, and co-workers. Do you recognize a dysfunction within any of these relationships that could be traced back to a power struggle or desire to control someone? Were these struggles present during your upbringing with one or both parents? Spend some time analyzing your own life starting with your current relationships, and work backwards from there. Take a good look at your childhood, as well. Were you allowed to follow your dreams, make mistakes, and learn from them? If you have children of your own are you allowing them the freedom to dream, to learn from their own mistakes? Can you identify how you participated in the power struggles around you? What role did you play? If you can identify areas of your life where you are either an instigator or a victim of power struggles—write them down. Awareness is the first step and from there you can work to develop a strategy to eliminate the behavior or address any associated negative emotions that might cause you to propagate this dysfunction in your own relationships.

Eliminating a controlling behavior isn't easy; recognizing them is tough, and eliminating them is even tougher. They have usually become habitual or they may have even developed into an aspect of your personality! But they are definitely unhealthy and your internal balance of energy suffers as long as they are in play. By becoming aware of where they exist in your life, and working to eradicate them you will begin to sense changes almost immediately. You will not only feel better physically (you will quite literally have more energy) and mentally, but your outlook on the world around you will begin to change and grow more positive. This will benefit you *and* those around you as you become a more positive influence in every aspect of your life. The world mirrors the energy you project!

Early on in my management career there was a woman engineer that worked for me on a highly classified defense project. She was competent, funny and quite intelligent, with a graduate degree from Cal Tech. She kept to herself most of the time though, and she didn't socialize very much with the rest of the team. One morning she came into work with a noticeable black eye and some pretty bad bruises on her arm. "I got into a fender bender," she explained, but something didn't seem quite right and I sensed there was more to the story. Later that afternoon as I walked by her office I noticed she was crying. "Are you okay?" I asked. She was initially embarrassed, but later confided that she had gotten into an argument with her husband, and that he had hit her. When I asked whether or not this was the first time, she reluctantly admitted that it was not. She explained that this was probably the most physically aggressive that he had ever gotten— usually it was verbal. She was clearly in an abusive relationship. I remember suggesting that she take the day off and go to see one of the counselors we had onsite to discuss the issue with them. It was definitely a situation that needed some professional advice or intervention. Several months passed and things seemed to be going better for her. She told me that she and her husband were in couple's therapy, and that they had made some serious changes within their relationship. In the end they did not stay together, but through therapy they were each able to identify their own issues and make healthier decisions about how to proceed.

There were obviously some pretty strong energy control issues taking place between the two of them. Even perfectly capable, intelligent people get caught up in these personal power struggles. We *all* participate in them on some level, and we *all* have some room for improvement in the way we interact with those around us. I did run into her again many years later at an airport somewhere in the middle of the country. I asked how she was doing, and as it turned out she was incredibly happy with the changes she had made in her life. The therapy had empowered her to some degree and increased her self-confidence. She had stopped participating in the control struggles with her husband and she was now (several years later) involved in a balanced, healthy, loving relationship.

The Dalai Lama also addresses control issues within relationships in his book *The Art of Happiness,* He says "Relationships are often the place where different types of power struggles and control activities play out... always to the detriment of the relationship."[30] Become aware of them in your own relationships; severe power struggles can have lasting negative effects, not just on your energy but on your mental and physical well being. If you are aware of this happening in your life, remember that you are responsible for managing your own energy. When you stop enabling and participating in the behavior, you are creating an environment (internally and externally) that will lead to greater balance and harmony of your energy with the people in your life. It's a difficult process, but a necessary one if you want to be free from these barriers to your happiness.

*Take a few moments and find a quiet place free from distractions where you can sit and objectively evaluate the elements of your life that bring you happiness, and those that cause you distress. Attempt to identify the sources of both. Take a pad of paper; write your thoughts down. Ask yourself what you want out of life, what you believe in, what your values are. How does this compare with what your parents or siblings want? How does this compare with the desires of your spouse or your children? Are you trying to gently guide your children in their lives or are you attempting to mold them (or even your spouse) in a direction that **you** want for them? Look for these more subtle versions of control struggles in your life, too.*

As parents we all want the best for our children but we may inadvertently allow control issues to play out as we seek to push them in one direction or another. Parenting is a tough job to say the least. Don't bully your children to obey you and follow your rules, provide them guidance, leadership and love and they will follow your lead much more freely. As you undergo the process of looking inward in order to assess these areas of your life, remember that we are all products of both our environment and our upbringing. Hereditary issues aside, we cannot escape the effects or the influence that the people who raised us have had on the development of our personality, psyche and consciousness. It helps to remember that you are influencing your children—just as your parents influenced you. Don't use your past, your parents or your childhood as an excuse for your actions, but rather use them as a source of knowledge in order to help you transcend any personal control issues or the further propagation of family dysfunction.

Those lucky enough to be involved in open, loving relationships will continue to freely share energy as they mature, letting the love grow. This type of relationship will be an ongoing source of energy renewal for everyone involved. These healthy loving relationships can be those we have with our spouses, children, our friends, and even our pets. Mutual love and affection is a great source of energy that builds upon itself; the more love we put out the more we get back. I've always been a dog lover, and over the years I've found them to be a great source of never-ending, unconditional love in return! A while back, I had a wonderful Yellow Lab named Colby—he was with me for over ten years, and he was a perfect example of how over the years, relationships may evolve and change, but your dog will always love you! Early on in my marriage (my kids were two and four years old at the time) we decided it was time to add a puppy to the family. The kids were just the right age, so we brought Colby home and he quickly became an integral part of the family unit. Every day when I would come home from work, both of my kids, my wife and Colby would greet me at the door when I arrived. As the years went on, my marriage matured and my kids got busy with their own lives, and eventually my best buddy Colby was the only one who still greeted me at the door when I came home from work. I loved that dog. He was always there, never too busy, and the novelty of greeting me never wore off for him—he was always thrilled to see me! He greeted me with the same enthusiasm, unconditional love and affection every single time, for his entire life. Pets are a wonderful way to boost the positive energy in your life.

The universe and everything within it is made up of dynamic, vibrating energy. Our relationships and the people around us are also important components of this universal energy. When we are balanced inwardly and in harmony with the world around us our energy flows freely. When we enjoy a healthy, balanced lifestyle; eat healthy foods; get proper sleep and exercise—this also serves to fuel our mind and body enhancing our internal flow of energy. Our emotions are also contributing factors. When we feel loved; feel a sense of purpose; feel like we are making progress in our lives, feel that we are valuable within our families, our jobs and our communities—our own internal energy flow is enhanced by this sense of well being. Positive states of mind, emotions, thoughts and attitudes will define the energy that we project and this positive energy is mirrored by the world around us. Synchronicity and coincidence give rise to meaningful interactions that move us forward along our life journey. When we feel a sense of purpose, and feel the world around us aligning with our attitudes and intentions, then our self-esteem and self-confidence is increased. Our sense of value and progress in life is strengthened and along with it, the level of our energy. As our overall energy is raised to a new level it helps raise the energy level of the people we cross paths with. Everyone benefits. When we participate in activities that inspire us, we also raise our positive energy level in a healthy way.

Have you ever been to a large group event that inspired you or raised your energy level in an almost tangible way? Perhaps a fabulous concert, a worship service or maybe even a great motivational seminar that left you feeling energized and elated? If so, then you can relate to what I am describing here… it is the result of your frequency of internal energy synchronizing with the entire group! Everyone's energy level feeds off each other.

Do you trust your own intuitions? Do you listen to your inner voice? Intuition is our subconscious mind trying to communicate an insight, or an awareness that our conscious minds have probably missed. Our conscious mind and our five senses are constantly "on" and they are in touch with most of the overt changes of energy around us and within us. Simultaneously, the subconscious mind is always running things behind the scenes, and also processing the more subtle changes in energy around us. Together they work in tandem to help us do most everything.

When we doubt our own direction in life, we distrust or ignore that inner voice (our intuition speaking to us,) or we are conflicted internally with indecision; our free flow of energy is blocked, and our energy can become depleted. We become lethargic, tired, listless, and unmotivated. Like a snowball rolling downhill, the negative energy in our life compounds. The cause for our malaise may not always be obvious, but the end result is this: Our brain becomes overloaded, the frequency of energy within our brains becomes out of synchronization with the energy around us, and the barriers to a free flow of energy get larger. This domino effect results in the depletion of our energy, a change in our brain chemistry, and the inherent feelings of depression and lethargy can creep in. Our brains, in effect, shut down and we are left "blocked" and unable to make a decision.

Dr. Dreher suggests, in her book, *The Tao of Inner Peace*, that in order to shift these negative feelings into a more positive realm and open up the flow of energy again; you have to center yourself, redirect your thoughts and attitudes, and refocus your attention on those areas of your life that bring you the most happiness and joy. You have to stay on track with positive thoughts and activities, and find your personal balance. She sagely advises, "Never confuse your center with the roles you play."[31]

Have you ever had a situation at home or at work where you have a mountain of work ahead of you, you're on a tight schedule, and you just don't know how to begin? It can feel so daunting and "big" that you don't know *where* to start… so you do nothing at all. You can waste time fretting that you'll never be able to handle the task in front of you because you're feeling so overwhelmed… but as a result you simply create a self-fulfilling prophecy.

The simplest solution is to take a step back, take a deep breath and climb the mountain, one small step at a time. Stop the cascade of events, and look at the challenge from a different perspective. The major challenges and conflicts in your life, including that project that seems so overwhelming, can be broken down into smaller, simpler pieces, and that way you can deal with the pieces—one at a time. By changing your mental attitude and redirecting your focus away from the negative "I **can't** *do this" to the more positive "I* **can** *do this" you will change your brain chemistry, increasing the positive flow of energy, and improving the balance of energy throughout your entire body. When you unlock the tension in your mind and your body and begin to relax—the world around you becomes much clearer. Don't forget to take some time to breathe and get in touch with your inner voice as well… you may find that you have an intuitive solution to the situation lying just beneath the surface of your consciousness. You'll begin to see your challenges and the task at hand from an entirely new perspective.*

Following our intuition and paying attention to the more subtle messages in our lives takes practice, but it gets easier with time. This process can easily be hindered by too much "noise" from our internal or external environment, so it is important to take time each day to quiet our minds. This quiet time will help to offset the deluge of sensory input we are continuously exposed to, and allow us to connect more effectively with our subconscious mind and our inner wisdom. As we learn to really listen to our intuition—we are literally training our brains to "see" differently—not just our external reality but our internal reality as well. We don't just wake up one morning and suddenly we're rewired. It takes effort, practice and focused introspection. It's an active, ongoing process that takes commitment on a daily basis.

So, start listening to that inner voice; look for the energy in your life with more than your five senses; use your sixth sense—your *sense of connection* to fill in the blind spots. "See" with all of your being and trust your intuition. Strive for a balance in energy between your internal and external realities. Become aware of the energy flow around you and you will see amazing changes in your life as your energy is synchronized with the positive energy that is all around you. Keep your mind focused on your life questions and the world will present the answers to you. Stay intent on your goals and objectives and your consciousness will direct the flow of energy in a way that will align the world around you in and enhance the probability of your success. Remember, your attitude, thoughts and intentions change the vibrational level of your energy, and the very frequency of the energy you project is mirrored by the world around you. Your conscious and subconscious minds are working on two different levels—so if you can synchronize them (keeping both your conscious and subconscious thoughts positive) and minimize your own internal conflicts, you will be able to see the world around you with much greater clarity. The energy you project will become far more cohesive, unified in harmony and focused.

It only makes sense that if we can influence the world around us, then we can change our lives for the better. We need to embrace the role we play as participants in creating our own realities, and manage our own energy levels responsibly. We can achieve our goals and objectives, and we can even overcome life threatening illness and injury with the very energy we possess. Through our positive thoughts, actions and intentions we are stacking the deck of cards in our favor. There are no guarantees in life, but we can certainly shift the probabilities our way by being more positive, and we can improve the quality of our lives along the way.

The world around us is changing at a rapid pace and along with it so is our sense of who we are and our role in the world. We can sense the changes that are taking place all around us every day. There is a change occurring in our global awareness, our sense of our connection with each other throughout the world, as well as with nature and with the environment. I believe this increasing awareness underscores the connections of this vast network of energy and leads us to this conclusion: We can, indeed affect our health, the health of the world around us, and influence our physical reality by changing our thoughts, attitudes, and intentions. Given the global situation right now—time is of the essence, and the positive world changes we desire will occur far more readily and more rapidly when we are in a place of balance and harmony within ourselves, and therefore with nature and with the universe itself.

Chapter Nine
Change Yourself and Change the World
◞◟

This truly is an amazing time in the evolution of the human race. We can no longer say that we live in a world where we are isolated as countries, cultures, or individuals. Science and technology have evolved in radical ways, confirming our connection to all that exists. Research papers being published by the quantum physicists of today sound incredibly like the teachings you will find of the ancient Eastern religious masters and philosophers. Our perceptions of the world and our connections to each other have certainly changed.

The growth of our knowledge in the field of psychology has also undergone a radical evolution. In the first few decades of this century, behaviorists believed the actions and interrelationships of the human species to be merely driven by instincts, cause and effect, action and reaction, and stimulus and response functions. The world of the human species was considered to be isolated, where each individual person was treated as an entity disconnected from the external physical world, driven in behavior by primitive needs. This paradigm is much like the old view of our isolated "Earth is the center of the universe" concept of the world (promoted by Newton) that initially prevailed in the scientific communities back in the 17th century and continued right on through to the first few decades of this century. This "disconnected" concept even held true in the approach of Western medicine as well until just recently. Illness and disease were typically considered to be isolated problems within the human body and were treated as isolated components of the whole by the medical community. This is drastically different from the traditional holistic approach of Eastern medicine— which treats the body as a whole and utilizes the energy flow and connections throughout the entire body during the treatment process. At long last, this "mind, body, spirit" approach typical of Eastern cultures has found its way into the Western world and is now becoming quite commonplace.

We can learn much from our history books on this subject. From the 1950's through the 1970's psychologists and behaviorists made great strides and discoveries in the areas of consciousness, perception, and human interaction. The veil of isolation was gradually being lifted, and many of the concepts promoted on the other side of the world by Eastern philosophers were finding their way into the research being performed by Western psychologists. Radical questions were being asked about how we experience our physical reality and what role our consciousness plays in our interactions with other people, and it was a time filled with speculation and postulation. Psychologists of that era ascertained that we view our exterior physical reality with our five senses, our brain interprets what we sense based upon our experiences, and we put these experiences into context in order to form thoughts, reasoning and ultimately actions. They believed that our actions were predicated upon our learned behaviors and the patterns we developed throughout our life experiences. It was originally thought that we simply reacted to different stimuli in our environment, and we just went through life in "cause and effect" relationships, playing out the behaviors we learned along the way. Many famed psychologists set forth a variety of interesting theories about human behavior, some suggesting that our ability to reason is what sets us apart as a species from other living organisms A myriad of assorted theories were thus created to describe how we as a species interact with our physical reality and with each other.

Carl Jung was the first psychologist to suggest that synchronicity occurs in our lives as a product of our consciousness interacting not only with other people, but also with the other elements of our physical reality. Jung believed that we possess a psychological wholeness embodied in our consciousness that moves us to realize our true potential. He suggested that, "In our early years of development we are primarily focused on our interactions with our external world. As we mature and gain increased insight and awareness, our journey is turned inward, consciously and subconsciously seeking a simplification to our lives, our relationships and a more centered self."[32] He described this inward journey as becoming "self-actualized" and he believed that as we become increasingly self-actualized through maturity and introspection the synchronicity in our lives will *increase,* guiding us along our inward journey.

Jung was also the first to discuss the power struggles that exist in our lives as a "subconscious mechanism designed to keep our normal scripts alive and flourishing as a means of self protection." He went on to suggest that "We resist growth and new experiences at the most important junctions in our lives because we are subconsciously sticking to our learned scripts, both those that we have carried forward from our upbringing as children, and those we developed as we matured through adolescence, and early adulthood."[6] While Jung didn't necessarily correlate these power struggles to our desire to control the energy flow of our physical reality, he did draw an astute correlation between the effects of synchronicity in our lives and the "excited" energy state of our minds. He also offered great insight about the relationships between our conscious and subconscious minds and our ability to affect change in our physical reality.

In the late 1980's and 1990's, explorations into our consciousness began to accelerate in earnest and paralleled the new discoveries in the field of quantum physics. The British biochemist Rupert Sheldrake postulated that life is surrounded by what he called a "morphogenic field," a field of energy that manifests our intentions and desires in our physical reality. While many scientists of that era considered Sheldrake's concepts radical (he is a firm believer in telepathy, among other things, and has done a great deal of fascinating research on the subject) and further believed his studies to be at the "fringe" of science, his ideas are now being increasingly embraced and adopted in this decade by philosophers, physicists, and biologists in emerging theories of energy and consciousness! Sheldrake theorized that our internal and external environment can motivate "jumps in the human evolutionary chain—where traits, physical skills, or intelligence levels make small but profound leaps forward." He says, "These leaps forward of human potential give rise to unique individuals, such as Einstein, who go on to make radical discoveries that move humanity forward in larger evolutionary steps that transcend existing human mental or physical boundaries."[33]

Sheldrake describes this "morphogenic field" as an energy field that surrounds and connects all living organisms. He suggests that this field is a conduit for intuition, for communication and a higher energy level that serves to allow ideas to be shared at a subconscious level. As Sheldrake explains, "This conduit is responsible for the many major discoveries that occur coincidentally at the same time across the globe. These discoveries are often of such magnitude that they have moved our knowledge and experience of ourselves and the physical world around us forward by great strides."[34]

Interestingly, Malcolm Gladwell discusses this very thing in a 2008 New Yorker magazine article about Nathan Myhrvold (formerly Chief Technology Officer at <u>Microsoft</u>) and his "Idea Factory." As Gladwell suggested, many researchers of scientific history contend that simultaneous discovery of inventions is the norm. Throughout history ideas have been discovered at the same time… even big ideas. Gladwell writes:

They found a hundred and forty-eight major scientific discoveries that fit the multiple patterns. Newton and Leibniz both discovered calculus. Charles Darwin and Alfred Russel Wallace both discovered evolution. Three mathematicians "invented" decimal fractions. Oxygen was discovered by Joseph Priestley, in Wiltshire, in 1774, and by Carl Wilhelm Scheele, in Uppsala, a year earlier. Color photography was invented at the same time by Charles Cross and by Louis Ducos du Hauron, in France. Logarithms were invented by John Napier and Henry Briggs in Britain, and by Joost Bürgi in Switzerland. There were four independent discoveries of sunspots, all in 1611; namely, by Galileo in Italy, Scheiner in Germany, Fabricius in Holland and Harriott in England.

The law of the conservation of energy, so significant in science and philosophy, was formulated four times independently in 1847, by Joule, Thomson, Colding and Helmholz. They had been anticipated by Robert Mayer in 1842. There seem to have been at least six different inventors of the thermometer and no less than nine claimants of the invention of the telescope. Typewriting machines were invented simultaneously in England and in America by several individuals in these countries. The steamboat is claimed as the "exclusive" discovery of Fulton, Jouffroy, Rumsey, Stevens and Symmington.[35]

How could such stunning developments, inventions and advancements possibly occur simultaneously throughout the world by chance? They could not. It is not by chance, but by coincidence—meaningful coincidence. *These concurrent events occur because of our natural connection to the universe and to each other—through the lattice of energy—via the Higgs field—the network that connects us all together.*

By the late 1990's the concept of our interconnectedness was pretty well established and accepted within both the scientific and psychological communities. In spite of this awareness, in the last decade alone, we have seen global environmental events, natural disasters, wars, terrorist acts, and economic strife push humanity to its limits. For most of this—we as a species are entirely to blame. While these events are tragic and much human life has been lost, perhaps they can serve a broader purpose. Perhaps they can serve as a catalyst to unite us together with a common goal for change. We have had enough destruction, devastation and conflict, and we, as a human race, have begun speaking out on an unprecedented global level. We want change… and we are demanding it of our world leaders. Perhaps the most recent award of the coveted Nobel Peace Prize to U.S. President Barack Obama speaks to this point directly! The world is ready for change. Significant efforts and energy, synchronized in frequency throughout the world are now being combined together to solve some of the most challenging problems the human race has ever faced. It is through these common goals and this collectively focused and harmonized energy that we will overcome our challenges and thrive as a species.

There is a vast body of research that has shown that our willpower, our intentions, thoughts, and attitudes have a much greater influence on our lives than was previously thought. For example, when projected through prayer, our thoughts have a tremendous impact on the healing process, pointing to the powerful effects of our intentions, the ability of our minds to change our physical reality, heal our bodies of sickness or injury, and recover our souls... "prayer is the most common complement to mainstream medicine, far outpacing acupuncture, herbs, vitamins and other alternative remedies."[36] These concepts, along with clinical and experimental data from psychologists and scientific researchers of the time, served as the foundation for many of the studies and much of the research that is now taking place in precognition, telepathy and mind control. While some of this research has proven inconclusive, much of what was discovered has served to validate and strengthen the current theories in mind/body connection. Today these fields of study and research include experts in the areas of physics, biology, and the many medical disciplines, as well as new areas such as Noetic Science, which focuses on research of the human mind. Together these fields continue to push our understanding of the power of the mind forward. Interestingly, the culmination of the work and knowledge that has amassed across these varied disciplines, particularly in the last twenty years, validates the existence of an energy field that is generated by our consciousness, one that has been shown to be capable of healing the body, engaging with our physical reality and shaping it according to our intentions.

The major discoveries in relativity theory and quantum mechanics have also shown us repeatedly that *all* matter in the universe is energy and that this energy is interconnected across a vast network—a network that facilitates instantaneous communication.

The Higgs Boson and the field that it creates, is theorized to be the underlying particle that makes this all possible. The psychology, medical, and related scientific communities have validated the existence of our consciousness and the energy fields that are created as a product of our thoughts, intentions and attitudes. We ourselves have all experienced this interconnectedness with the universe, with our physical reality, and with other people: when we meet someone and feel somehow instantly connected, like we've met them before; or when we seem to finish sentences for someone or complete their thoughts. These are everyday examples of this interconnectedness of energy. We have all been aware of coincidences in our lives, where we seemed to be at the right place, at just the right time and something good or meaningful came of it. You've no doubt experienced cases of déjà vu, where you seem to have repeated an experience, or perhaps seen a glimpse of the future. These are all relatively commonplace examples that each of us can relate to directly, and they also serve to validate the concept of the power of the mind to affect our physical reality. When we think positively we uplift ourselves, we uplift others around us and the world aligns with our energy. This isn't an accident, this is a product of the energy field we project—it's real!

In these changing times there is a growing awareness that we need to break down old barriers and habits of thought in order to make some very real changes not just in our own lives, but in the world around us. At the same time, many of us feel powerless to effect this change. How do we change the world when we can't event change the oil in our cars? Right now the country and much of the world is in upheaval and there is a great deal of fear and negative energy all around us. So, how do we move past all of this negativity? How can we possibly change the world as individuals? The answer is simple really. We don't change the world all at once; *we change the world one person at a time.*

Start with yourself and make changes within that will deliver results almost immediately. Take responsibility for your thoughts and intentions and your interactions with those around you. Keep your energy positive and you will contribute to global change through your own growth and awareness. It may take a while for us to pull the world out of the mess we have made and restore some semblance of balance, but this is our chance—and every minute counts. The challenges we face now on a worldwide basis are an opportunity for us all to re-prioritize, to grow as individuals and connect as a global community.

Remember, as we become increasingly aware and open to our potential and possibilities, our attitudes and intentions will synchronize more closely with our internal energy field. Our energy field becomes increasingly stronger as it aligns with the frequency of energy around us, and as it does, it amplifies the energy on both sides of the interaction, increasing our awareness and heightening our sense of intuition. When we are excited and happy it impacts the people around us and their energy level rises as a result of ours, which in turn elevates our own energy level even higher... as well as that of anyone else we are interacting with. It's contagious!

As you change yourself, the world around you will automatically respond and change, too. It increases exponentially—with one person influencing the next and that person the next, and so on. You manifest your own wave of energy that ripples across the universe! Collectively everyone's energy is elevated, frequencies of energy are aligned, and your positive thoughts and intentions just spread from one person to the next. In this way, you can and *do* influence events and shape your physical reality according to your attitude and intentions. Granted, the message of your intentions will be diluted the farther it propagates, but a broader change to the awareness level of all that have participated in the energy exchange will be effected. Your energy will ripple outward just like the waves created by the rock you threw into the still lake. Your contribution is essential, it *matters*, and each step you take along the path of your journey through life leads you to a broadening of your perspective, an increase in your knowledge and experience, an elevation of your vibrational energy level, and a new, higher level of awareness for everyone.

Carl Jung theorized that "with each one of the changes we make in ourselves that serves to increase our awareness and wisdom we move closer to a higher state of consciousness."[32] Because we are all intrinsically connected and we automatically influence each other, over time we will actually help to advance the human species forward through our *own* evolutionary path, moving toward a higher state of consciousness as a species, one person at a time, much like climbing that mountain one small step at a time!

Make a personal commitment to be positive and integrate these positive thoughts, intentions and attitudes into your life every day. You can use meditation, prayer or quiet introspection (whatever works best for you) to still your mind, and integrate these practices into your daily routine. Make it a priority to find a healthy balance in your life. Written affirmations and visualization are valuable tools to help increase your focus and strengthen your resolve to achieve the goals and objectives you have established for yourself. Focus your entire being on achieving your true potential, one step at a time. With this single-minded focus on your desires and intentions, your full energy will be integrated into your consciousness, and your energy projection will be clear and powerful. With the positive actions you take in your life, you are changing the path of your own future reality.

We live in a dynamic energy responsive universe; we project energy just as others around us project energy. This energy always seeks to reach a balance and harmony because in nature, energy automatically seeks to synchronize with other energy. This is the real essence of the law of attraction. Pay attention to what type of energy you are projecting, and become aware of the energy around you, too. Avoid the control issues and power struggles that so often exist in our interactions with others. Recognize them when they do occur and learn to release them. Try to avoid negative energy in your life but understand that this negative energy is in the natural order of things, too. While you cannot avoid it entirely, you can minimize your exposure to it and counter it with your own positive energy. Enhance your positive feelings and energy by doing the things that make you happy and bring you joy. You will find that by enveloping a negative energy with your positive energy it becomes neutralized and dissipates. If you remain centered and focused, you can avoid absorbing any of it at all—it will pass through you quickly and with no lasting effect.

How can we strengthen our own energy, and learn to focus it? Meditation is one of the best techniques I have found. Eastern prophets believe that our core energy is weak until we open ourselves up to the energy of the universe around us. As we become centered and more confident—the flow of our internal energy increases. As our flow of energy increases, so does our connection to the vast conduit of energy within the universe. "Eastern mystics who have attained a state of enlightenment (typically through meditation) reach a transformational state of mind that enables them to move beyond the restrictions of time and space."[9] Prayer (much like meditation) can lead us to a similar state of mind. The goal of either approach is to block out all of the external noise in our minds and harmonize the frequency of energy within our entire mind, with clear focus of our intentions and desires. These processes literally synchronize the energy within our brains, the neurons firing by the millions in a common frequency. When we synchronize the energy in our own minds, we significantly increase the projection powers behind our thoughts and attitudes.

When you calm your mind, as you do in meditation, you mentally push away not only the noise and clutter that exists in your external physical reality, but also the noise and conflicting thoughts of your internal mental reality. By calming your mind, you are also calming your body, and through a process of gradual, successive relaxation; random thoughts that are passing through your mind will slow down and then cease altogether. At that point the vibrational level of energy in your brain begins to synchronize; first in one hemisphere, then the other and finally across both hemispheres together. This synchronization process further increases your state of relaxation. Your sense of self begins to dissipate, the sensations in your extremities disappear, and you become increasingly "aware." It is in this state of relaxation and calmness that you can direct the flow of energy within your mind and clearly focus on the subject of your intentions. As your state of relaxation increases—so does the synchronization and vibrational level of your energy, and your control over this energy will internally peak, allowing you to direct the flow of energy as you wish simply by guiding it. Your state of consciousness shifts to a new level. Your connection to the energy flow of the universe is opened up and you may feel as though you are experiencing an out of body sensation.

Meditation works, and anyone can attain this level of relaxation with practice. The benefits to your life will be nothing short of miraculous. I was just fourteen years old when I first started this kind of deep meditation. With no training whatsoever (other than a very basic understanding of the concepts). I intuitively began a gradual process of relaxation and focus that allowed me to enter into deeper and deeper states of relaxation, and heightened levels of consciousness. My motivation was huge. As I shared with you earlier in this book, I was lying in a hospital bed paralyzed from the neck down... with little or no other options. I decided to see how powerful my mind actually was—and I used it to heal my own body.

As I shared with you, I started out slowly, but I was soon able to meditate in a very deep state for hours at a time, with one single focus—to heal my body. At the point of my deepest relaxation, when all sense of my body and the external world melted away, I would focus all of my energy on the area of my neck and spinal cord that was injured. I envisioned the cells of my body physically healing the wounded area, bathing the injured areas in waves of healing positive energy. A little over a month later I was able to stand, and I had regained all of the sensation below my neck. Several weeks after that, I walked out of the hospital on my own. To this day I have virtually no residual effects from that injury! Some might call this a miracle—or an act of divine intervention.... Perhaps, but for me it is also a *validation*, as pure as it can get, of the true power of the mind.

You could argue perhaps that this was a fluke, and if this was my one and only experience with this true raw power, I might be inclined to agree. But nine months after that diving accident, I was involved in an equally life threatening car accident—I found my only choice was to try to repeat the very same process. To my amazement I was met with very similar results. In less than a month, I was back on my feet and walking out of the hospital once again. On those two occasions, I was able to use the power of my mind, this very energy that I have been talking about throughout these pages, to do precisely that. I used the power and energy of my mind to change my physical reality. I also had the help of many doctors, family and friends; and their faith and support lifted me up and strengthened my conviction. In many ways I was fortunate to learn at such a young age how powerful we really are. What I learned back then has guided me throughout my entire life, and replayed itself in many far less dramatic scenarios. I came into adulthood knowing that I could do anything, and that I could create my own reality, and I have. Those two experiences increased my awareness on many levels and they also inspired my lifelong search for greater knowledge and understanding. Those accidents changed the course of my journey, they changed my life forever.

There may very well be times in your life when you feel that you just don't have the strength to endure, or to overcome the challenge or the adversity before you. At times like this don't rely on your energy alone. Involve the love and support of the people around you to lift you up and freely share their energy. As their energy synchronizes with your own—you will see a multiplying effect of your own energy. This is precisely how you get through those times. Love and support is one of the most powerful sources of energy and one of the most self-sustaining. Embrace it and watch your life change.

With the global and economic challenges we are currently experiencing, it is far too easy to fall into a negative state of mind as soon as we wake up. We have only to turn on the morning news, or simply open the newspaper and we are completely bombarded by reminders of the eroding world economy, the conflicts and wars in the Middle East, terrorist attacks, and the deteriorating state of our environment! Unfortunately, the negativity is everywhere, and it is impossible to avoid it completely. I'm not suggesting that we live in denial about what's happening in the world, but I do suggest that we minimize our exposure to the negative barrage of news and information in order to keep a more positive mindset. So, until we can change things, we have to turn it off, shut it out, and minimize it as much as possible.

But, avoiding negativity won't stop it completely, so you have to make a conscious effort to fill your life with all of the positive energy that you can. Look in the mirror each morning and tell yourself about all the good things in your life! Who cares if you seem a little crazy? Make Post-it notes and put them around the house in conspicuous places with affirmations of the positive things in your life, do the things that you enjoy, get a dog, fall in love! Balance the negative energy with positive energy. Remember that the natural order of the universe is cyclical, which means that some negative energy is appropriate. You can choose to maintain a positive attitude, keep the energy flow in your life positive, and remind yourself daily about the good things in your life.

Look for the people, things and experiences in life that inspire you. Keep your sprits high and your mind open, and remember to embrace the coincidences in your life—they can be an important source of renewed energy that will keep you moving forward along your life's journey. When you run into obstacles or adversity in your life, just stay positive, and keep your desires and intentions at the forefront of your mind. Don't get caught up in the small details of any conflicts or adversity. It's important to keep the bigger picture in mind. Push on through your adversity. If you are faced with something in your life that feels just too big for you to handle or overcome on your own, then break it down into smaller pieces and enlist the support and love of your family and friends.

When we open ourselves up to a higher vibrational level of energy, a heightened state of consciousness, we experience an overall shift of our thoughts and attitudes, and we see a dramatic increase in our level of energy. Our spirits lift and others around us respond similarly.

You can use your energy as a positive inspiration for others as well. By freely giving away your positive energy you will in turn be the recipient of far more than you project. Remember that the energy of the world will mirror *your* energy field. When two such fields come within close proximity of one another and they synchronize in frequency, both parties receive an increase above and beyond their own individual contributions. Our quantum energy patterns move in harmony with each other and synchronize with our physical reality in exactly the same way.

The world we live in is changing, and, as a result, so are we. It is the natural order of things—*change is necessary*, the universe is cyclical, and it attempts continuously to find a balance in the flow of energy. The Taoists call this the balance of the life force "Yin" and "Yang", representing the opposing forces in the balance of nature, the masculine and feminine, the light and the darkness, the positive and the negative. They are connected yet separate in many ways—one always comes with the other and the cycle continues. As we go through life we will always have ups and downs, we will always have our own cycles. Balance is important, so we need to accept the negative just as we would accept the positive– but keep our focus on the positive. Negative events and situations can always be useful for contrast and comparison, and they help us to appreciate the more positive aspects of our lives.

Be positive and your life will change. Find your center, decide what you want out of life, and think and act accordingly. You need to shed any misguided beliefs about who or what you are, and internalize the fact that you are indeed powerful in your own right. Accept responsibility for the fact that you yourself determine who you are now and what you become through your own thoughts, intentions, and actions. Because this is important I will re-iterate: Your choices and decisions determine your path in life.

The world around us is exactly as we would have it be. We become what we think about, and the world around us reflects the energy we project, positive or negative. The universe is filled with energy, all interconnected in a vast array, and we are not only connected with this energy, we also *contribute* to it. We can be buoyed up by it or we can be brought down by it. This energy and our physical reality both respond to our attitudes, our intentions, and bend to meet our expectations. The world unfolds before us as we would expect it to. As we begin to center ourselves and open ourselves up to the great potential; to the possibilities the world has to offer, we will be lifted in spirit. Our vibrational levels of energy will increase and we will begin to flow with the natural order. As we continue to remain open and positive, our mind and spirit will become increasingly calmer. We will see the world around us in an entirely new and enhanced way; sounds will become clearer, our vision crisper, our thoughts more focused, and our bodies invigorated. The power struggles in our lives will dissipate because we see them for what they are and rise above them. The world is indeed changing, and we may very well be in a natural "negative" cycle. But we *can* change it—one person at a time, starting from within. Together we will reverse the trend, and reach a higher level of balance, happiness and security. *Remember, change yourself... and change the world!*

Chapter Ten
Life Comes Full Circle

There *is* a power buried deep within each of us, an energy that will enrich our lives, and in turn enrich the lives of those around us. Once we discover and unlock this incredible energy for ourselves, our lives will change. These are the facts: Each of us has the ability to affect our physical reality, influence the people in our lives, and heal our own bodies. By changing our attitudes and intentions we can literally change our own reality. Our attitudes, thoughts, and intentions are all manifested through our consciousness—and we can choose to keep them positive. As our minds become focused millions of neurons in our brains are simultaneously firing, entrained on the very focus of our thoughts, attitudes, and intentions. A small but very powerful electromagnetic field is generated within our brains as a result of the electrical energy created by the synchronous firing of these neurons. This energy, enabled through the connective forces of the Higgs field, moves outward into the world around us at frequencies unique to our thoughts and attitudes—faster than the speed of light, and our energy interacts with the energy fields of other people and elements of our physical reality. Through this interaction, the world around us will attempt to synchronize with the frequency of energy that we project, seeking to find a balance, a harmony, which is the natural order of nature. *By doing so, the world mirrors the energy we project. We become what we think about, and the world around us conforms to our attitudes and intentions. In turn, the world becomes what we expect it to be. We literally co-create our own reality!*

As we change our attitudes and intentions towards a more positive direction, our lives will begin to move forward in a way that reflects our hopes and expectations. Our awareness of this energy that exists within each of us and all around us—flowing through everything—is crucial to our evolution as a species. Through the power of our attitudes and intentions and the energy field that each one of us projects we can change our physical reality, heal our bodies, and transform the world around us as we desire. By elevating our own positive energy levels, and increasing our awareness of the influence we actually have over our own physical reality, *we become the key to changing the world—one person at a time.*

The effects of our positive attitudes and intentions create an expanding wave of positive energy that propagates farther and farther outward instantaneously. We've compared this to the expanding circle of waves that result when a stone is tossed into a calm lake. Just as a there are dualities in nature; there is also a duality in the energy we project; it possesses the properties of both a particle and a wave simultaneously. Metaphorically, we become the stones creating waves of a new found awareness on the lake of humanity. Our individual and collective positive thoughts, attitudes, and intentions will ultimately create a tipping point of global awareness within our lifetimes that will improve the world for this generation, the next generation, and the generations beyond. This tipping point will occur as the energy within each of us and throughout the world synchronizes; through our unified intention of improving the human condition on our planet.

Throughout this book I have tried to increase your awareness of the potential we each possess to affect our own physical reality. By peeling back the layers of scientific, psychological and mystical insights, I've attempted to lead you to a place where you can draw your own conclusions about our unique capacity to change our lives as well as the lives of those around us—simply by changing our attitudes and intentions. As you begin to correlate the information and the personal experiences I have shared in this book with your own life, beliefs, and circumstances, you may well reach a new level in your own stage of enlightenment. I hope that my story and these words have inspired you in some way to embrace your own power. Every single one of us has the power to change our own lives for the better, no matter the circumstances, no matter the challenge. We have the power within ourselves, the power within our own minds, to make our lives and the world around us what we want it to be. We have the power to positively change our lives right now, to alter our future, to heal our bodies, to change our world.

The key… it's you. It's the very energy you posses, the frequency of positive energy you project, and the conscious decisions you make every day of your life that will begin to positively change you and impact the world around you from this point forward. You hold the key inside of you; it's your thoughts, attitudes, and intentions. Be positive and your life will change!

Scientifically, we now know that the world around us and everything in it; all matter (both organic and inorganic) is made up of molecules and atoms, and beyond that—at the subatomic level, of protons, neutrons, and electrons—which are actually tiny bundles of (particle/anti-particle) energy in a constant state of vibrating motion. All of this energy is intricately woven together and interconnected together across the entire universe. We now know that the universe and all it contains were created billions of years ago from a single explosion (the "Big Bang") of highly dense energy, and that this massive explosion of light projected this energy outward, in ever expanding cosmic waves. In fact, we also know that the universe is still expanding and still moving outward—even now! All of the energy that currently exists came from this one event, and it never goes away or ceases to exist, it just changes from one form to another. This energy is cyclical; it has peaks and troughs, just like waves on the ocean. Everything in nature (including the universe itself) follows these natural rhythms, these cycles, and each one of us also follows these natural cycles. The universe will continue to contract and expand indefinitely. It was created from a singularity that collapsed inward upon itself, to the point where, at the subatomic level the opposing forces of energy (fundamental forces within each of the fundamental particles that formed this super dense matter) led to a violent explosion outward called the "Big Bang." All the galaxies in our universe have been created as a result, and at the center of each galaxy is a black hole that may eventually lead back to a gradual inward collapse of all the energy that exists around it, and so it goes. The cycle of expansion of our vast universe may eventually reverse its course and begin a contraction process, billions and billions of years from now, and the universe will once again collapse inward upon itself, resulting in a new explosion of energy and the re-birth of a new system. The universe and all energy within it will ultimately come full circle.

We see this cycle of contraction and expansion in nature, and our lives follow a similar path. We go through many cycles in our lifetimes, we have ups and downs, positive and negative cycles, we are born and eventually we will die. It's a fact of nature, a part of the cosmic order. For every death a life springs forth… the energy never goes away, it only changes form. The universe and all that exists, is in a constant state of renewal… and life goes on.

What's really important is that we maintain a balance of this energy, and live our lives in the best way we possibly can while we are here. Life, as we know it, is just too short to live with regrets, too short to live with negativity, or with anger towards ourselves or anyone else. You can make a difference in your own life, and in the lives of those around you. Live your life in a positive way and live it to your fullest potential! You have the power to make the changes you want to see in your life, you always have.

Don't just think you can do it, *know* you can do it. You *do* have the power and control over your own life and can begin to make positive changes for yourself right now! Understanding this is the first step, but you must also take action. Act upon your intuitions, pay attention to the coincidences and opportunities the world presents to you, and *act* upon your decision to change your life. Use the tools you have learned here to help you find your inner balance and flow: meditation, visualization, and affirmations—all of these techniques will enhance your focus and strengthen your convictions. As you look at the world around you; remember that you are connected to it in a very intimate way. All that you are made of; all of the cells, the atoms, and energy within you is the same energy that is inherent in everyone and everything around you, and in everything that exists in our universe. Your energy and the frequency of positive energy you project out into the world around you can improve your life and change your world forever.

We live in a fascinating time where our knowledge of the world around us, on a cosmic level and subatomic level, is expanding at an ever-increasing rate. We are also seeing a widespread movement towards a higher plane of consciousness, and a greater understanding of our roles in this world. The convergence between Western science and Eastern mysticism is accelerating to a point where, in our lifetimes, we will surely witness the concrete scientific confirmation of both the creation of life, and the unity and interconnectedness of the universe. Many believe the discovery of the Higgs Boson will ultimately lead us to this very conclusion along with the unified "Theory of Everything." We are getting much closer to being able to answer some of the fundamental questions that have been asked over the ages—regarding who we are and where we came from. Eastern wisdom encourages us to find within ourselves the answers to these questions. While science has typically strived to discover answers empirically through experimentation, Eastern religious philosophies have always maintained a focus on the inward journey of investigation seeking wisdom through introspection, meditation and enlightenment as a means to gain answers to the deepest spiritual questions.

It's interesting to note that both approaches have increased our knowledge of ourselves, the world around us, and the interconnectedness that we have with each other and the universe. Indeed, the more we search within ourselves, our external world, and the subatomic world; the more we discover that each of us holds the very essence of the universe within us. It is deep within each and every cell and atom we are made of… it's the elemental energy that *all* of creation is constructed from. This pure energy is the essence of the universe, the essence of nature; the essence of the energy in each of us… the essence of creation!

To look deep inside yourself; to look closely at your motivations, your moral and ethical character, your beliefs and your desire for change in your life; is to begin the process of making lasting and positive changes that will alter your life forever. Through the act of introspection and the adoption of a more positive attitude, you are already changing your own reality, changing the frequency of your own energy; changing your future. This is the starting point for positive changes in your life. The link between your energy field and the reality of your life is undeniable. Your ability to influence your life and those around you through the projection of a positive energy, in harmony with the world around you, has been proven scientifically, and validated by over 2500 years of documented wisdom and history in Eastern philosophies. The energy that will change your life is within you. As you change your thoughts, attitude, and intentions the frequency of energy you project will be mirrored by the world around you. As you think so shall you become... so, *be positive!*

Know that each one of us holds
The very essence of the energy of the universe, of all space and time
Deep within us, indeed, the very essence of God.

—Rich Wood

Epilogue

The process of writing this book has turned out to be quite a journey, much like my life itself has been. As I formulated, researched, drafted, and finalized each of the chapters, I discovered that I couldn't really treat each one of the chapters as separate entities but rather as aspects of the whole. The information doesn't break down into neat little packages by the very nature of the content—and therefore, each chapter overlaps with the next and they are all interconnected—just like the fundamental messages of this book.

As we begin to understand that the energy within each of us is connected to the vast amount of energy in the universe, we progressively grasp the full weight and meaning behind its power to impact and change our lives. I've placed these ideas into context with my own experiences, and shared with you many vignettes from my own life. I firmly believe that I am not unique—life has not given me any more opportunities than anyone else, but I did start paying attention to them at a fairly young age! If you look around with a fresh perspective, you will probably find that you have had many similar coincidences, challenges and opportunities in your life. Of course, hindsight is always the clearest way to see the lessons that were there for us in the challenging situations we've experienced... but hopefully my story will help you to look at them as opportunities for growth, and inspire you to become more aware of the synchronicity at work in your life as well. I hope that my personal experiences will also help you to appreciate your life, your family members and your own personal journey in a new way. We all have "teachers" around us all the time—and there is something to be learned from every experience and every single person we come in contact with.

Most of all—I sincerely hope that you will be inspired by the facts contained within these pages, and become empowered to explore the potential that is within you. You are powerful... and you can do anything you set your mind to!

Please visit my website, www.bepositivebooks.com to learn more about integrating these ideas into your life, and look for my IPHONE/IPAD apps coming in July.

About the Author

Rich Wood currently resides in Santa Barbara, California with his wife Mary, four cats and of course, his Yellow Lab, Brody. His daughter McCall will graduate from Berkeley this year with her degree in Architecture, and his son A.J. is a junior at UCLA studying Political Science. Following a very successful career in the Aerospace and Defense markets as an entrepreneur, engineer, and business development and marketing executive, Rich took a mid-career sabbatical in 2004, during which time he honed his flying skills, becoming a skilled flight instructor and commercial pilot. He is currently running two Multi-national manufacturing, warehousing, and logistics companies; distributing products worldwide. Rich continues to maintain his security clearances supporting the Department of Defense and Intelligence markets as a consultant through a specialized consulting firm in Southern California. In his "spare" time you'll find him skiing, hiking... or daydreaming in the local Sierra Mountains.

For those of you who are wondering about his blood type, as you might have guessed... it's "B Positive!"

I'VE ARRANGED A SPECIAL OPPORTUNITY FOR YOU TO BE MENTORED AND INSPIRED BY MY GOOD FRIEND, JACK CANFIELD!

You probably know him as the creator of the *Chicken Soup for the Soul* book series. And in his latest bestseller, *The Success Principles*, Jack and his coauthor Janet Switzer teach 64 principles the world's top achievers use to create the life of their dreams.

Now you can be mentored by Jack for FREE...
With The Success Principles Private Mentorship Program!

LOG ON TO WWW.THESUCCESSPRINCIPLES.COM AND REGISTER NOW...

You'll be sent a complete welcome kit via email along with FREE course materials...plus you'll receive unique life planning tools from Jack Canfield and *The Success Principles* coauthor Janet Switzer.

DETERMINE WHAT YOU WANT TO ACCOMPLISH THIS YEAR...

It's your chance to dream big...from your ideal career to your perfect lifestyle to having the home of your dreams to enjoying the relationships, people and pursuits you love.

LET JACK & JANET PERSONALLY GUIDE YOU IN MEETING YOUR GOALS...

Listen and learn as Jack and Janet walk you through a unique combination of audio training, daily inspiration and easy-to-apply action steps for getting where you want to be.

GET INVITED TO JACK CANFIELD'S NEXT SUCCESS EVENT WHEN YOU OPT-IN!

Opt-in today, and you'll be invited to meet Jack in person at one of his renowned international success symposiums! Opt-in at TheSuccessPrinciples.com now to receive upcoming dates and cities.

LEARN JACK CANFIELD'S SUCCESS PRINCIPLES & GET HIS PRIVATE MENTORSHIP PROGRAM... FREE!

Suggested Reading

1. Bell, C., *Comprehending Coincidence*, Chrysalis Books, 2000
2. Bohm, D., *Wholeness and the Implicate Order*, Boston: Rouledge and Kegan Paul, 1980
3. Bohm, D., and Hiley, B., *On the Intuitive Understanding of Non-Locaility as Implied in Quantum Theory*, Brickbeck College, University of London, 1974
4. Capra, F., *The Tao of Physics*, Shambala Publications, Inc., 1999
5. Capra, F., *Chronology of the Development of Quantum Mechanics*, unpublished paper prepared for the Physics/ Consciousness Research Group, J. Sarfatti, PhD, Director
6. Dossey, L., *Recovering the Soul*, Bantam, 1989
7. Dossey, L., *Healing Words*, Harper Collins, 1993
8. Dreher, D., *The Tao of Inner Peace*, Harper Collins, 1990
9. Eckhart, M., *Treatises and Sermons of Meister Eckhart*, Hippocrene, 1983
10. Eddington, Sir Arthur, *The Nature of the Physical World*, New York: McMIllin Company, 1929
11. Einstein, A. and Infield, L., *The Evolution of Physics*, Simon and Schuster, 1961
12. Einstein, A., Podolsky, B., and Rosen, N., *Can Quantum-Mechanical Description of Physical Reality Be Considered Complete?*, Physical Review, 47, 1935, 777

13. Engel, G. et.al., *Evidence for Wavelike Energy Transfer Through Quantum Coherence in Photosyntheitc Systems*, Nature 446:786-6, 2007

14. Feynman, R., *Mathematical Formulation of Quantum Theory of Electromagnetic Interaction, in Schwinger*, J. (ed.), Selected Papers of Quantum Electrodynamics, Dover, 1958

15. Finkelstein, D., *Beneath Time Exploration in Quantum Topology*, unpublished paper

16. Finkelstein, D., *Past-Future Asymmetry of the Gravitational Field of a Point Particle*, Physical Review 110, 1958, 965

17. Govinda, L. A., *Foundations of Tibetan Mysticism*, New York: E.P. Dutton and Co., 1960

18. Hameroff, S.R., *Information Processing in Microtubules*, Journal of Theoretical Biology, 98:549-61

19. Hawking, S., *The Universe in a Nutshell*, Bantam Books, 2001

20. Hesienberg, W., *Physics and Beyond*, Harper and Row, 1971

21. Hesienberg, W., *Physics and Philosophy*, Harper and Row, 1958

22. HH Dalai Lama and Howard C. Cutler, M.D., Penguin Putnam, Inc. 1998

23. Hillman, J., *We Had a Hundred Years of Psychotherapy—and the World's Getting Worse*, Harper, 1992

24. Jung, C.G., *The Collected Works of C.G. Jung*. Vol 10 Princeton University Press 1969

25. Jung, C.G. *Synchronicity*, Princeton University Press, 1973

26. Koestler, A., *The Roots of Coincidence*, Random House, 1972

27. Lao-Tzu, Tao Te Ching, Alfred A. Knopf, Inc, Random House, Translation by D.C. Chou

28. McFarlane, T., Einstein and Buddha, *Seastone*, 2002

29. McFadden, J., *Evidence For an Electromagnetic Field Theory of Consciousness, Journal of Consciousness Studies*, 9:23-50, 2002

30. Peat, F. D., *Synchronicity: The Bridge Between Matter and Mind*, Bantam Books, 1987

31. Penrose, R., *Emperor's New Mind*, Oxford University Press, 1989
32. Penrose, R., *Shadows of the Mind*, Oxford University Press, 1994
33. Redfield, J., *The Celestine Vision*, Warner Books, Inc., 1997
34. Shan, G., *A Primary Quantum Model of Telepathy*, The Parapsychology Association Convention, 2004
35. Stapp, H., *S-Matrix Interpretation of Quantum Theory*, Physical Review, D3, 1971, 1303
36. Suzuki, D.T., *Swedenburg: Buddha of the North*, The Swedenburg Foundation, 1996
37. Swedenborg, E., *Scientific and Philosophical Treatises*, Swedenborg Foundation, 1991
38. Talbot, Michael, *Mysticism and the New Physics*, Penguin Books, 1981
39. Targ, R. and Puthoff, H., *Mind Reach*, Delacorte Press, 1977
40. Tegmark, M., *Importance of Quantum Coherence in Brain Processes*, Physical Review E 61:4192-206, 2000
41. Verhoeven, M., *Buddhism and Science: Probing the Boundaries of Faith and Reason, Religion East and West*, Issues 1, 2001
42. Vivekanda, S., *The Complete Works of Swami Vivekananda*, Advaita Ashrama, 1989
43. Von Franz, M., *Psyche and Matter*, Shambala Publications, Inc, 1992
44. Watts, A.W., *Way of Zen Mentor*, New American Library, 1957
45. Zukav, G., *The Dancing Wu Li Masters*, Harper Collins, 2001

Bibliography

1 *Emoto, Masaru, Love Thyself The Messages from Water III, Hay House, 2004*

2 *McFadden, Johnjoe, Evidence For an Electromagnetic Field Theory of Consciousness, Journal of Consciousness Studies, 9:23-50, 2002*

3 *Davidson, Richard. M.D., et. al., Long-term meditators self-induce high-amplitude gamma synchrony during mental practice, Paper 2004, The National Academy of Sciences*

4 *Hawking, Stephen, The Universe in a Nutshell, Bantam Books, 2001*

5 *Ellis, John , J.S. Hagelin, (SLAC) , Dimitri V. Nanopoulos, Keith A. Olive, M. Srednicki, (CERN) . Supersymmetric Relics from the Big Bang, SLAC-PUB-3171, Jul 1983. Published in Nucl.Phys.B238:453-476, 1984*

6 *Jung, Carl, The Collected Works of C.G. Jung. Vol 10 Princeton University Press 1969*

7 *Lederman, Leon and Teresi, Dick, , The God Particle: If the Universe Is the Answer, What Is the Question?, Dell Publishing, 1993*

8   *Bell, Craig, Comprehending Coincidence, Chrysalis Books, 2000*

9   *Capra, Fritjof, The Tao of Physics, Shambala Publications, Inc., 1999*

10 *Peale, Norman Vincent. The Power of Positive Thinking, Ballantine Books Edition and Prentice-Hall, 1982*

11 *Cruz, Julia , Surviving Cancer with Faith, Focus and Cyberknife, Beth Israel Deaconess Medical Center newsletter November, 2009*

12 *Bennett, C.; et al. (2003a). "The Microwave Anisotropy Probe (MAP) Mission". Astrophysical Journal 583: 1–23. doi:10.1086/345346*

13 *Hinshaw, G.; et al. (2007). "Three-Year Wilkinson Microwave Anisotropy Probe (WMAP1) Observations: Temperature Analysis". Astrophysical Journal Supplement 170: 288–334. doi:10.1086/513698*

14 *Einstein, A., Podolsky, B., and Rosen, N. Can Quantum-Mechanical Description of Physical Reality Be Considered Complete?, Physical Review, 47, 1935, 777*

15 *Higgs, Peter, Broken Symmetries and the Masses of Gauge Bosons, Phys. Rev. Lett. 13, 508 (1964)*

16 *Chung-liang, Al Huang, Embrace Tiger Return to Mountain: The Essence of Tai Ji, Real People Press, 1973*

17 *Finkelstein, David, Beneath Time Exploration in Quantum Topology, unpublished paper 1976*

18 *Targ, R. and Puthoff, H. Mind-Reach, Delacorte Press, 1977*

19 *Bell, J. S. , On the problem of hidden variables in quantum mechanics, Rev. Mod. Phys. 38, (1966)*

[20] *Bell, J. S. , Introduction to the hidden variable question, Proceedings of the International School of Physics 'Enrico Fermi', Course IL, Foundations of Quantum Mechanics (1971)*

[21] *Hesienberg, Werner, Physics and Beyond, Harper and Row, 1971*

[22] *Zukav, Gary, The Dancing Wu Li Masters, Harper Collins, 2001*

[23] *Naess, Arne, The Shallow and the Deep, Long-Range Ecology Movement, Inquiry 16: 95-100 (1973)*

[24] *Capra, Fritjof. The Web of Life: a New Scientific Understanding of Living Systems, Anchor Books, NY 1997;*

[25] *Maturana, Humberto and Francisco Varela, The Tree of Knowledge, Shambala Publications, 1998*

[26] *Lao Tzu, Tao Te Ching, Translation of the Ma Wang Tui Manuscripts by D.C. Lau, Everyman's Library, Alfred A. Knopf, 1994*

[27] *Seaton, Jerome and Hamill, Sam. (1998). The Essential Chuang Tzu. Boston: Shambhala Press*

[28] *Govinda, L. A. Foundations of Tibetan Mysticism, New York: E.P. Dutton and Co., 1960*

[29] *Redfield, James, The Celestine Vision, Warner Books, Inc., 1997*

[30] *HH Dalai Lama and Howard C. Cutler, M.D. The Art of Happiness, Penguin Putnam, Inc. 1998*

[31] *Dreher, Diane, . The Tao of Inner Peace, Harper Collins, 1990*

[32] *Jung, C.G. Synchronicity, Princeton University Press, 1973*

[33] *Sheldrake, Rupert; Stanislav Grof, Editor (1984). Morphic Resonance. seventh Conference of the International Transpersonal Association, Bombay: SUNY Press, Albany*

[34] *Rupert Sheldrake (2005,. Morphic Fields and Morphic Resonance: An Introduction, Paper, February 2005*

[35] *Gladwell, Malcolm. May 2008, New Yorker article about Nathan Myhrvold's "Idea Factory."*

[36] *Researchers Look at Prayer and Healing, Washington Post, March 24, 2006*

BUY A SHARE OF THE FUTURE IN YOUR COMMUNITY

These certificates make great holiday, graduation and birthday gifts that can be personalized with the recipient's name. The cost of one S.H.A.R.E. or one square foot is $54.17. The personalized certificate is suitable for framing and will state the number of shares purchased and the amount of each share, as well as the recipient's name. The home that you participate in "building" will last for many years and will continue to grow in value.

Here is a sample SHARE certificate:

THIS CERTIFIES THAT

YOUR NAME HERE

HAS INVESTED IN A HOME FOR A DESERVING FAMILY

1985-2005

TWENTY YEARS OF BUILDING FUTURES IN OUR COMMUNITY ONE HOME AT A TIME

1200 SQUARE FOOT HOUSE @ $65,000 = $54.17 PER SQUARE FOOT
This certificate represents a tax deductible donation. It has no cash value.

YES, I WOULD LIKE TO HELP!

I support the work that Habitat for Humanity does and I want to be part of the excitement! As a donor, I will receive periodic updates on your construction activities but, more importantly, I know my gift will help a family in our community realize the dream of homeownership. **I would like to SHARE in your efforts against substandard housing in my community!** *(Please print below)*

PLEASE SEND ME _____ SHARES at $54.17 EACH = $ $_____

In Honor Of: _____

Occasion: (Circle One) HOLIDAY   BIRTHDAY   ANNIVERSARY

    OTHER: _____

Address of Recipient: _____

Gift From: _____ *Donor Address:* _____

Donor Email: _____

I AM ENCLOSING A CHECK FOR $ $_____ PAYABLE TO HABITAT FOR HUMANITY OR PLEASE CHARGE MY VISA OR MASTERCARD *(CIRCLE ONE)*

Card Number _____ Expiration Date: _____

Name as it appears on Credit Card _____ Charge Amount $ _____

Signature _____

Billing Address _____

Telephone # Day _____ Eve _____

PLEASE NOTE: Your contribution is tax-deductible to the fullest extent allowed by law.
Habitat for Humanity • P.O. Box 1443 • Newport News, VA 23601 • 757-596-5553
www.HelpHabitatforHumanity.org

Printed in the USA
CPSIA information can be obtained
at www.ICGtesting.com
JSHW082158140824
68134JS00014B/307